MW00415614

# power
# mood

## Unlock Your Confidence, Transform Your Life & Command Your Value

### SAM DEMASE

ROCK
POINT

Brimming with creative inspiration, how-to projects, and useful information to enrich your everyday life, quarto.com is a favorite destination for those pursuing their interests and passions.

© 2023 by Quarto Publishing Group USA Inc.
Text © 2023 by Samantha DeMase

First published in 2023 by Rock Point, an imprint of The Quarto Group, 142 West 36th Street, 4th Floor, New York, NY 10018, USA
T (212) 779-4972  F (212) 779-6058  www.Quarto.com

All rights reserved. No part of this book may be reproduced in any form without written permission of the copyright owners. All images in this book have been reproduced with the knowledge and prior consent of the artists concerned, and no responsibility is accepted by producer, publisher, or printer for any infringement of copyright or otherwise, arising from the contents of this publication. Every effort has been made to ensure that credits accurately comply with information supplied. We apologize for any inaccuracies that may have occurred and will resolve inaccurate or missing information in a subsequent reprinting of the book.

Rock Point titles are also available at discount for retail, wholesale, promotional, and bulk purchase. For details, contact the Special Sales Manager by email at specialsales@quarto.com or by mail at The Quarto Group, Attn: Special Sales Manager, 100 Cummings Center Suite 265D, Beverly, MA 01915 USA.

10  9  8  7  6  5  4  3  2  1

Library of Congress Control Number: 2022944671

ISBN: 978-1-63106-935-2

Publisher: Rage Kindelsperger
Creative Director: Laura Drew
Managing Editor: Cara Donaldson
Editor: Amanda Gambill
Cover Design: Laura Drew
Cover Illustration: Tristram Drew
Interior Design: Kim Winscher

Printed in China

This book provides general information on various widely known and widely accepted self-help concepts that tend to evoke feelings of strength and confidence. However, it should not be relied upon as recommending or promoting any specific diagnosis or method of treatment for a particular condition, and it is not intended as a substitute for medical advice or for direct diagnosis and treatment of a medical condition by a qualified physician. Readers who have questions about a particular condition, possible treatments for that condition, or possible reactions from the condition or its treatment should consult a physician or other qualified healthcare professional.

For the gals and nonbinary pals.

# CONTENTS

# INTRODUCTION

**POWER MOOD MUSIC**

DO IT
BY CHLOE X HALLE

0:48                                                −3:27

I wrote this book for you. Yes, you! I see you. This book is a treasure trove of straightforward, actionable tips that I have employed in my career and life—things I've learned along my journey as a woman in the workplace. And someone who started her career with low confidence, but who now teaches self-advocacy, confidence cornerstones, and negotiation skills to other women.

Allow me to be your hype-woman, and when you're done reading this book, you'll be your own. I'm not going to lie; I wrote this book for the girls, and I'm woman enough to admit it. That's not to say my tips don't apply to and work for everyone—they very much do! However, I *am* a woman, and that fact informs my life and career. I relate deeply to other women because we share the same experiences. This is reflected not only in the data we'll look at later, but also in the way my online community resonates with the stories I share.

The Power Mood community on social media is more than 80 percent women. This is by design because they are who I want to reach! I'm doing this for the girls, and I'm unapologetically pro-lady. It's who I am, and it's what I know. I've found power in my womanhood and want to equip others with the means to harness that same power. Nonbinary, genderqueer, and agender folks, I see you, too, and I champion you. Thank you for being here.

To the men who will hopefully read this book, as well, hi there! My tips also apply to you. This book will likely be eye-opening for you in terms of what women are up against in the workplace. The fact is, the career experiences of women and nonbinary folks differ remarkably from those of men, particularly cis white men. For women, and especially women of color, it's an uphill battle. We're attempting to thrive in a system that wasn't built for us.

This context is important to keep in mind as you read this book. We will look at data about the gender pay gap, lack of women in leadership roles, and the challenges that women of color face in this system.

Men can be workplace feminists too, and if you believe in equal opportunities for men and women in the workplace, you're a workplace feminist. Spread the message far and wide! As men, you are important allies on our journey to workplace equity.

If something you read strikes a chord, I encourage you to open up a conversation with both the women *and* men in your life. Share what resonated with you, what you've learned, and offer an empathetic ear in that dialogue. It feels great to be seen and heard in this way, especially when it involves things that aren't frequently talked about, like a lot of the topics I cover in this book. Listening and learning is a great place to start, and I appreciate you being here.

I'm not a proponent of "girlboss" culture in the traditional sense. First, the term has an infantilizing, condescending quality to it. Moreover, it comes from an era where, yes, women had a platform, but only the privileged white founders. The term was also associated with "hustle culture," i.e., work as hard as you possibly can without prioritizing your mental health.

I firmly do not believe you have to be hustling 24-7 to be of value. It's complex because, at its height (2014–2016), "girlboss" did empower and resonate with so many women. And if it made some feel empowered to create change for the better, that's important to acknowledge. Ultimately, though, the sun is setting on the term, and I think it's for the best—but she sure did have her moment.

To put it simply, I stand for giving the girls the tools they need to thrive in a system that's broken. I am an intersectional feminist on a lifelong journey of learning. I strive to be inclusive in my work and am firmly aware of my own privilege as a middle-class raised white woman. I know that I'll make mistakes on this journey, but I will continue to do the work to learn and unlearn.

However, this book was not written through the lens of a victim because I don't consider myself to be one. Sure, I've been through some less-than-ideal situations, but it was through those that I learned a ton about the corporate system. And now, I teach others how to approach their careers with confidence and clarity.

Learning and deploying self-advocacy changed my life and career. I spent my early days kind of shaky-confident. I just DIY'ed my way through, throwing stuff at the wall to see what would stick. I went with my gut and did what felt right. Was I unsure of myself at times? Absolutely! However, it seemed better than the alternatives.

Like many of us, I've always worked in male-dominated industries, which I viewed as both an opportunity and a challenge. A lot of odd things have happened to me (we'll get to those later), and I didn't always perceive them as sexist at the time. In hindsight, however, I realize I was being gaslit pretty consistently. Nowadays, I have the confidence, skills, and language to go to bat for myself.

The first time I thought that something wasn't quite right was when I interviewed for my first professional job post-college. Having worked in hospitality since I was fifteen years old, I was familiar with the vibes and the environment. During my interview for my first full-time role, the male interviewer asked me if running a kitchen was really for me, since I'm a woman and everything. Oof!

I was flustered at the time, but I couldn't quite place my discomfort. All I could think was that I wanted to move on as quickly as possible. He asked *me* an inappropriate, sexist question, and *I* was the one who felt embarrassed, uncomfortable, and wanting nothing more than to teleport out of there. It felt simultaneously familiar, frustrating, and terrifying.

I responded by nervously saying I'd been working in restaurants for several years and was excited about the opportunity. I kept the conversation moving, ensuring it remained positive, but I didn't acknowledge the blatant sexism in his question. If that were me *now*, I certainly would have had some different words for that interviewer; probably something along the lines of, "Why do you ask? Are you implying that women can't succeed in this role? If so, please elaborate."

A short time into my tenure at that job, a customer asked me to get the manager, to which I replied, "Hi, I'm the manager. How can I help?"

"Not you," he said. "The manager. I need to speak with the man in charge."

"The woman in charge is right here," I said through gritted teeth, while giving him a fake smile. "And she's the only manager on duty right now."

I wish I could say this only happened once, but it actually occurred on several occasions. This was the beginning of a series of similar (and even worse) experiences as a woman at work. However, these all ultimately just served as fuel to start my own business and write this book.

When I first got word that I had a book deal, I was so excited to share the news! My friends were so hyped and proud of me. Their enthusiasm and love were palpable, and it was a beautiful moment to share with them. In contrast, when I informed certain family members that I had some exciting news, their immediate response was, "Oh my gosh, you're pregnant!"

This was disheartening, and also awkward, because I was then in the uncomfortable position of letting them down. It took all the steam out of my joyful announcement. In fact, I felt like a balloon slowly deflating. In the moment, I chose to ignore the statement and just proceed with my news. The reaction was subdued, to say the least. There was some excitement, but it was unmistakably shrouded in disappointment. They were visibly let down, and I felt like crap.

After that, I changed the way I shared my book news. Instead of opening with, "I have exciting news," I would say, "I have exciting news related to my business." This curbed any potential confusion and eliminated any disappointment that I, in fact, was *not* pregnant.

As I reflected on this (it happened more than once during my book announcements), it gave me more motivation to write this book, and specifically, about that moment and how I felt. I'm hopeful for a future in which we don't immediately assume that if a woman has good news, it's that she's pregnant or engaged. When a man says he has exciting news, do we jump to those same conclusions? I think not.

In addition to overcoming workplace feminism, a core theme of this book is also about overcoming imposter syndrome, or, as I like to think of it, entering your power-mood era, which is the direct opposite of imposter syndrome. I struggled to overcome the latter as I wrote this book. I thought to myself, "There are so many career books out there. Do we really need another one?"

However, I also remembered that of the top twenty career books on Amazon, only one was written by a woman, so yeah, we obviously need more. Do we need more career books written by women of color? Yes! How about more written by disabled women? Also, yes! Do we need one written by me? Yes, because if this book resonates with even one person, it's a win!

This book is all killer, no filler. It is raspberry jam packed with gold nuggets, and no chapter is dispensable. Like a Beyoncé album, I'm talking zero skips, baby. All the info is juicy, a lot of it is eye-opening, and a ton of it is empowering. When it comes to your career and navigating the system, I've left no topic untouched and no secret untold.

There are a few things you can expect from this book, and I want you to be as hyped as I am, so here's a sneak peek. First, it's divided into the following three parts:

1. **Conjuring:** How to land the job and salary you want and deserve.

2. **Crafting:** How to make an impact at that job, build relationships, and get promoted.
3. **Cultivating:** How to build your leadership presence, cultivate your ideal work environment, and be a mentor.

There are also a few fun, recurring segments throughout this book because who doesn't love those? Frankly, they're one of my love languages. These true stories and helpful quick tips are tucked inside each chapter and relate to the respective theme of each. Here's a preview of what you have to look forward to:

- **Power Mood Music:** At the start of each chapter, I recommend a song that replicates the mood of that chapter. Have it on in the background as you read or listen to it after you read the chapter. You can even create a playlist of all the songs after you finish the book. Every song is a certified banger and will champion you as you step into your power mood.
- **Underused Power Moves:** These quick, actionable tips are based on things I wish I'd known earlier in my career. This is the stuff that isn't talked about nearly enough.
- **The Fearless Careerist:** Bold-ass mastermind maneuvers that yield massive results. Buckle up!
- **Corporate Chronicles:** Juicy personal stories from my eventful ride of a career thus far, which ultimately led me to write this book.
- **Power Memos:** Short, power-boosting quotes to repeat, remember, and share.
- **Recruiter Secrets:** Insider knowledge from the hiring side of the desk.

If you follow me on social media (hi, friends!), you know that my style is very straightforward, self-assured, and brief. Like my thirty-second Instagram and TikTok videos, my tips in this book get straight to the point and are immediately actionable. You can put this stuff into practice right away.

Many of the chapters use a three-step framework to guide you through the theme and get results. I did this intentionally, because it's an effective, explicit, and fun way to learn and retain information. I encourage you to take notes as you read and highlight the parts that resonate. You can even take photos and text them to your friends. There are a lot of gems in here that I can't wait for you to discover.

My primary goal with this book is to make the essential techniques for thriving in the corporate system readily accessible. You'll learn how to:

- Write a resume that highlights your achievements so you can land a better job.
- Crush an interview with fearless confidence.
- Negotiate your salary like a pro.
- Stand up to a toxic boss.
- Implement healthy boundaries at work.

I want to ensure that this info—and much, much more—no longer remains hidden. It should be available to all of us, not just the few who happen to be "in the know." That is precisely why I started posting videos on my Instagram about how to hack the corporate system. I want women everywhere to be able to employ these strategies and see incredible gains.

We'll investigate some important data in the coming chapters regarding the percentage of women (and women of color) in management roles and CEO seats. As you can probably imagine, the numbers are not ideal.

I want to see that data start to look different. I want to see us represented, and I want my book to be part of the positive change that happens when we advocate for ourselves. While we wait for the system to change, we can take it into our own hands.

To give you another little preview of what's to come, I've included some feedback from my Power Mood community. All of the folks below have implemented my advice and landed some major wins:

> "Your negotiating tips helped me get a $25K pay increase, 20 percent bonus, and sign-on bonus!"
>
> —*Danielle P., Blandon, PA.*

> "Can I just tell you, you helped me negotiate a $115K position, and I couldn't be prouder."
>
> —*Kayla M., Washington, D.C.*

> "I've officially accepted a new position, making double (that's right; double!) my current total compensation."
>
> —*Kelsey M., Chicago, IL.*

> "Sam, because of you I felt confident and cool while negotiating a new salary that is $21K higher than my current salary! I think the work you do is so important to empower the girls, gays, and theys."
>
> —*Michele M., Denver, CO.*

> "I just got a raise three times what I was originally given during my review in February. I based my conversation on my performance stats and asked if I was being paid equitably. Thank you for being a truly amazing resource!"
>
> —*Julia O., Alisa Viejo, CA.*

> "I have been absorbing your content and ordered the resume guide and cover letter guide. I just landed a dream job I never otherwise would have felt ready to apply for, and got a 43 percent increase in salary from my previous role, too! Thanks for what you do!"
>
> —*Elizabeth H., Houston, TX.*

"I start Monday making $10,000 more a year than I did with the company I was at for fifteen years. Watching your videos was a huge confidence boost! Thank you."

—*Kelly H., Kingman, AZ.*

"Today, I successfully negotiated a job offer for a $20K base salary increase (and a first-time six-figure income), and I owe it to your tips! Thank you for doing what you're doing—your videos have made me feel empowered, and make me want to empower all the women in my life! You're awesome and millennials need you!"

—*Shannon S., Mont Clare, PA.*

"I decided to apply for jobs and, in the final stage, used your tips and phrases to negotiate pay and other factors. I got a 55 percent increase in my base salary, a senior title, and a later start date, so I can take a holiday between jobs. Thank you so much for your tips and advice!"

—*Vandna B., London, U.K.*

"Your tips on negotiating made it possible for me to get a 100 percent wage increase! I went into the meeting with my boss knowing my worth and market value. After listing all the tangibles I've produced over the last twelve months, they couldn't deny that I was more than deserving of an increase."

—*Claire W., Roseville, MN.*

Now, it's your turn. It's time to conjure your ideal career path, craft your goals, and cultivate your ideal work environment. After reading this book, you'll be fully equipped with all the tools you need to successfully advocate for yourself in the workplace and in your life.

*Your* success story is next!

# PART I
# CONJURING

Confidence begins with knowing and embracing who you are. To conjure up your power mood and ideal career path, you first have to be intentional about getting to know yourself. This section will help you discover and celebrate your superpowers. We'll also explore where confidence comes from, and how to inhabit the power mood mindset. From there, we'll dive into how to expertly navigate the core elements of your job search from building a resume and interviewing, to salary negotiation.

The common theme that runs through Part I is that preparation breeds confidence. When it comes to the job search and interview process, most of your success can be found in the preparation phase. We'll approach all of these topics with a foundation of confidence and a propensity for self-advocacy.

Each element we'll cover builds on the previous. If you have a resume that shines and highlights your accomplishments, you'll be proud walking into any interview. Next, you'll learn how to approach those conversations with a newfound confidence and belief in your value and skillset. By the time you get to the negotiation phase, you'll be fully prepared to advocate for what you're worth and command your value.

After implementing the advice in this section, your only possible outcome will be to get the job and the salary you want!

# CHAPTER 1

## THE POWER MOOD MINDSET

**POWER MOOD MUSIC**

RUNNING WITH THE HURRICANE
BY CAMP COPE

0:48                                                    −4:16

You know how you get outraged when something bad happens to your best friend? Most likely, you immediately defend them and offer some empathy, followed by recommendations of what they should do next. You are your best friend's fiercest advocate. If only you could give their toxic boss a piece of your mind! But, why is it so hard for us to do that for ourselves?

I have a remedy for this: have your best friend write your bio. This activity is based on a text exchange I had with my best friend. She was struggling to write a short bio for herself, so I wrote one for her, and it was epic.

I encourage you to do this with your best friend. You write theirs, they can write yours, and then you both share them. It doesn't have to be long—a few sentences is perfect. It's a great mood boost and will help you gain confidence. It also puts into perspective just how awesome you are—especially if you tend to undersell yourself. I really like this exercise as an initial step in defining your superpowers, which are an important part of your power mood.

So, what is a power mood, and how do you get one?

Well, your power mood originates in those moments that clarify your purpose. It's an individual expression that changes with you over time. As you figure out what motivates you, what you care about, and what you need to be your best self, your power mood grows.

When you discover your superpowers (the things you do better than anyone else) and use them to your advantage, your power mood grows. When you support and uplift other women, your power mood also grows.

Getting to know yourself and celebrating all of your beautifully unique qualities is part of the journey to finding your power mood. For example, I'm a quirky, oddball, nerd of a person, who is also a deeply committed consumer and referencer of niche pop culture, past and present. I love theater, elder music divas, and fine desserts. I have a vested interest in green tea, scented candles, and *RuPaul's Drag Race*. I have tight-knit chosen and biological families, both of which are a big part of my life.

In my free time, you'll find me arranging flowers, going to concerts, and dancing until I'm completely spent. I've also made a conscious decision never to hide any of this at work—I bring my whole self and fully recommend that everyone do the same.

Bringing your whole self to work is not only empowering, but it also enhances your quality of work. When you show up authentically, others will relate to you more profoundly. They'll gravitate to you and want to listen to what you have to say. Being genuine and vulnerable opens up the door to creativity and innovation. You harness your superpowers as you find comfort in the power of being yourself.

For me, it hurts to leave pieces of myself behind when I go to work because a lot of them are the very reasons why I work.

It's where my motivation lies, and it feels right to carry them with me. When you bring your whole self to work, it shines through in your confidence and the way you present yourself. We all approach it differently, and sometimes it varies daily. You don't have to bring it 100 percent every day—after all, you do need to save some for after work. Find a balance that feels right for you, as you bring more of your authentic self into your work.

I'm frequently asked how I can be as confident as I am. **Spoiler alert** (and I'm woman enough to admit this): I'm definitely not confident all the time. It's something I've had to work very hard on. I channel it for my benefit and the benefit of others when I need to.

Confidence is extremely personal—it looks and feels different for everyone—but it begins with taking the time to get to know who you are. What makes you, you?

On the journey of getting to know ourselves, it's easy to stress about the things that make us feel "different." However, these are the aspects of your personality that are actually your superpowers. This is where the root of your confidence lives. You are singular; nobody will ever do you better than you.

I don't believe that we can (or should) be confident all of the time. That's unrealistic and actually does everyone a disservice because we're all complex, emotional people. Humans need to feel their feeling, whatever those might be, but confidence is a decision! All you have to do is choose the moments when you need it, and then conjure it.

Choosing when to tap into your confidence and use it to your advantage is your power mood. You already have it; you simply need the tools, phrases, and tips from this book to fully unlock it.

Your power mood is advocating for the salary you deserve and getting it. It's also setting healthy boundaries that allow you to flourish in your work and your life.

Your power mood is recognizing the signs of a toxic boss and holding them accountable. And finally, it's you shedding the confines of people-pleasing and putting yourself first.

This book is your guide to finding your power mood, and we have a lot of ground to cover. The topics we'll look at aren't generally the types of things you learn in school or from your family, though. So, where the heck do we learn them? Why has this knowledge been gatekept?

These were the questions I asked myself before I started Power Mood. I still don't fully know the answers, but I think it has something to do with the "powers that be" not wanting us to have this information, so they can always have the upper hand. And to that I say, "Nope!"

By the end of this book, you'll know how to properly frame your resume so it highlights your achievements, how to interview and land the job, what to say during a salary negotiation to get what you're worth, as well as how to combat imposter syndrome, set healthy workplace boundaries, stop over-apologizing at work, and much more.

# THE FEARLESS CAREERIST
## SIGNS IT'S TIME TO FIND YOUR POWER MOOD

I haven't always been the "fearless careerist" I am today. There are so many obstacles on the path to confidence and success—especially for women—at times you'll want to shut it all out and take a nap. So, do that; rest is productive!

When you wake up, though, it's time to push forward, re-energized. And always remember, you are *not* alone! Every single one of us has been there. Below are 10 signs that it's time for you to find your Power Mood:

1. You're in a job that undervalues you.
2. You're feeling burnt out at work.
3. Your job isn't mentally stimulating.
4. You struggle to implement healthy boundaries.
5. You downplay your accomplishments.
6. You're drowning in negative self-talk.
7. You *always* put others first, but never yourself.
8. You don't believe you deserve success.
9. You have a hard time accepting compliments.
10. You apologize way too often, even when something isn't your fault.

# CHAPTER 2
## FINDING YOUR CAREER PATH

**POWER MOOD MUSIC**

THE LONG WAY AROUND
BY THE CHICKS

0:48                                                    −4:33

⏸
◀◀                                                     ▶▶

There isn't one dream job out there waiting for you; unfortunately, that is a myth. The truth is, there are many jobs that can fulfill you. In my opinion, the idea of the "dream job" is harmful. Those of us who never find it will feel like failures or like we're missing out. For many of us, life is our priority and a job is just a means to an end—it allows us to live the life we want to live.

The joy experienced from a job varies greatly from person to person. Some love their job and it becomes a large part of their identity, some don't enjoy their work but do enjoy the stability, while others fall somewhere in-between. All of these different feelings and experiences are completely valid and normal.

A great place to start when thinking about your career path is to identify your superpowers. Again, your superpowers are the things you're better at than anyone else. They are the areas in which you excel and thrive. Sometimes, there's an overlap between your superpowers and the things you enjoy doing, and sometimes, there isn't.

A decidedly nonexhaustive list of superpowers might include the following traits and talents:

- Being a compelling storyteller
- Being able to synthesize complex information
- Being an empath
- Being able to analyze a process, identify flaws, and improve upon them
- Being a creative force
- Being super detail-oriented
- Being a skilled researcher
- Being able to pitch and sell anything
- Being a compelling public speaker
- Bringing out the best in others
- The power of persuasion
- The ability to innovate and execute big ideas

Almost as important as identifying your superpowers is being able to articulate them in all of their profound impact and glory. The best way to do this in the context of a cover letter or job interview is to relate it to the job at hand. I call this "Name It and Proclaim It," and to do it, all you have to do is use specific examples from your experience.

For example, in an interview you might say, "One of my superpowers is innovating and executing big ideas (*name it*). In my last role, I created a program from the ground up, which increased customer engagement by 40 percent. I look forward to innovating and making an impact in a similar way here (*proclaim it*)."

Take some time now to think about your superpowers and write them down. Brainstorm some examples of how you've delivered on those superpowers. These will come in handy for cover letters, interviews, and as reminders of your greatness (and imposter syndrome antidotes). Even if you're just starting out your career, you already have innate superpowers because your life experiences and challenges have informed and built them.

Not sure what your superpowers are? I encourage you to take the CliftonStrengths Assessment or a similar career or personality assessment. There are many of them out there, including career aptitude tests, personality quizzes, enneagrams, Myers-Briggs, and more. This can be a great way to do some exploring and build some self-awareness. It might even bring something interesting to the surface that you never realized before. While these types of assessments and quizzes don't have the last word on highlighting superpowers, you'll likely discover some gems in the results that really strike a chord. Take what resonates and leave the rest.

My favorite assessments are those that help you discover and celebrate your superpowers. The CliftonStrengths is a thirty-minute assessment that helps you unlock and articulate your unique strengths, and it's a gateway to embracing your superpowers. It revealed to me my top five strengths: futuristic, strategic, maximizer, ideation, and relator. As I read through the detailed results, so much of it resonated with me. It identified the things I knew I was good at, but hadn't necessarily articulated in a specific way. It made me feel proud and confident to see my unique superpowers in detail. I also have superpowers that I recognize outside of that assessment, too, but it got the ball rolling for me. Our superpowers grow, evolve, and change over time, just as we do, so it's a good idea to revisit the assessment from time to time and reconsider your superpowers. You'll most likely be delighted to see how much you've grown.

Superpowers can sometimes be found in odd places. In fact, something you may view as a weakness could be a superpower. CliftonStrengths breaks down your strengths and places them in four distinct categories: executing, influencing, relationship-building, and strategic thinking. Some of the strengths within those categories include: individualization, adaptability, achiever, learner, positivity, focus, and more. There are boundless categories of superpowers outside of this, as well, such as creative, scientific, medical, technical, people skills, research, and support. Your superpowers are unique to you and should be celebrated. They can also be the key to unlocking your career path.

The intersection of your enjoyment of deploying a superpower and its value to an organization is the bulls-eye. The more you enjoy using your particular superpower(s), and the more an organization values them, the higher your chance of being successful and thriving in that job. The goal is for you to bring your favorite superpowers to an organization that deeply values those particular traits.

The chart below illustrates this concept:

Be open-minded and adaptable when it comes to your career path. You might change jobs more frequently than you thought, or even change course altogether and do something completely

| | | |
|---|---|---|
| **YOUR ENJOYMENT OF EXCERCISING YOUR SUPERPOWER** | High enjoyment and low value | Your ideal career path lies in this quadrant |
| | Low enjoyment and low value | Low enjoyment and high value |

High enjoyment and high value = your ideal career path, a.k.a., utilizing a superpower you enjoy and getting paid well to do so.

THE VALUE OF YOUR SUPERPOWER TO AN ORG.

different. For example, you might start in a corporate job, but then switch to freelance gigs or entrepreneurship, and then back to a corporate role. This isn't talked about enough, and I know a ton of people who operate this way, myself included. We put so much pressure on finding the one career that's right for us, and that is an outdated and limiting mentality. When I was a kid, I was never able to answer the question, "What do you want to be when you grow up?" I understand now that I wanted to be so many things, it was hard to answer that question because I didn't want to limit myself.

We grow and evolve, and gain new strengths and passions. We might get bored of a particular setting and crave change, and your superpowers qualify you for a multitude of careers. If you do find yourself making a big career change, keep in mind that as long as you have some transferable superpowers, your value goes up—not down—when you change careers. This is because you bring unique skills and experience to a team that it doesn't currently have. You add a tremendous amount of value so don't sell yourself short.

When you have an idea of a few careers or industries that interest you, talk to your friends, friends of friends, family members, and online connections. Ask them about their careers, how they got where they are, and what they enjoy about it. Come prepared with questions you want to ask, and take notes during the chat if it's helpful.

Here are a few examples of what you might want to ask them:

- What drew you to this career?
- What are your superpowers?
- What are you most proud of in your career?
- What is the work environment like?
- What is the most challenging aspect of your job?
- What is your work-life balance like?
- What are your career goals?

This may spark something that you hadn't considered before or affirm a career you were considering. It's important to talk to someone in that industry before you decide on a job. You need to get a sense of what the day-to-day will be like before you jump in. Use social media to research companies that interest you. Find out what their values are and see if they align with yours.

In terms of values, you'll need to define your own to discover the industries and companies with which you align. Consider how they take care of their teams, the work environment, sustainability, giving back, and anything else that's important to you. Companies vary widely on all of these fronts, even within the same industry. Check out their corporate website and read up on them. You should find sections on the company's culture, values, mission statement, benefits, and so on. Also, you can search the company on the Glassdoor website to get behind-the-scenes reviews from current and former employees.

It's also important to consider which type of work environment you thrive in: collaboration versus working solo, fast-paced versus deliberate, or a big team versus a tight-knit crew. Work environment also includes the option of flexibility, such as full- or part-time remote work. If you know you won't thrive in a full-time office job, seek out remote opportunities. If you're unsure which type of office environment you want or need, you might have to try something just to see if it works. As you evolve in your career, this will become clearer and clearer. You might first have to learn from experience what you *don't* want in a work environment before you can strategically explore other options.

If you've had full- or part-time jobs, or internships, take an inventory of what you liked and didn't like. Consider the job duties, supervisors, and coworkers. How did it feel to work there? Think about the wins and challenges, and how you felt in the moment. Did you feel empowered? Challenged in a good way? Exhausted? It's important to analyze your past experiences so you can make informed decisions about your future.

There are online courses out there on just about everything, from digital marketing to web design and investing. Some are free, and some are not, but you might discover a concept you're excited about. Take an introductory course, and if you're intrigued, you can pursue it further.

Another way to find a satisfying career path is to think about your life in general. If you want to prioritize your personal or family life, consider what it would look like if you framed your job as a "side hustle." For example, you might want your life to include all (or some) of the following:

- Tons of travel
- Time for hobbies and creative projects
- The option to live anywhere you want, and move any time you want
- Being a dog, cat, or other pet parent
- Living near family and friends
- Raising a family
- (Insert your vision here.)

Your priorities will also likely change at different stages of your life and as you evolve as a person. You might have a period of time where you crave a highly social job that, for a while, really fulfills you. After a time, however, you might find yourself needing to break away from that and do something different, which is totally okay and valid.

Of course, the ability to approach work in this way requires privilege. Many of us are working jobs that don't mesh with our desired lifestyle; however, all is not lost. You have options! Remember, your superpowers are not only suitable for one specific career, they'll work in many. It's all about how you articulate those superpowers and link them to your desired job in a meaningful way. I'll cover this in the next chapter. And later, you'll also learn in detail how to set boundaries and cultivate your ideal work environment, so that your personal life is always at the forefront. Career change for the better is not only possible, it's achievable, as long as you have the right strategies.

# CHAPTER 3
## THE RESUME REMODEL

**POWER MOOD MUSIC**

THRIVING
BY DIET CIG

0:48                                    −3:45

Career confidence starts with your resume: if it highlights your accomplishments, you're setting yourself up for major success. However, more often than not, I find that people's resumes do not tell their story accurately. This is especially true for those of us who hesitate to take credit for our work.

I'm here to tell you, take all the damn credit. It's yours! I don't care if you filed paperwork eight hours a day at your previous gig, you did it astonishingly well, with ferocious attention to detail, and with a 100 percent accuracy rate!

Did you know that women usually only apply for a job when they feel they meet 100 percent of the job requirements, while men do so even if they only meet 60 percent? This eye-opening statistic, which originated from an internal report conducted at Hewlett Packard, has been quoted far and wide, including in the *Harvard Business Review* in 2014.

In response, I recommend you start channeling the audacity of the mediocre man! Apply for jobs even if you think you're underqualified—always shoot your shot. Don't take yourself out of the race before it's even begun. After all, applying is zero risk, so create opportunities for yourself.

Something I love doing is looking at someone's current resume, asking them a few key questions, and then turning that same resume into one that screams to potential employers, "Your search ends here! I'm the one you've been looking for!" To you, it should say, "This is the resume of someone whose salary should be at least 25 percent higher."

The way I see your resume versus the way you see it is akin to the concept we dove into earlier, when I recommended having your best friend write your bio. We tend to minimize our own accomplishments, or even be completely blind to them. Sometimes, it takes an outside perspective to reframe what you see as just doing your job into the accomplishments that they truly are. I'm going to teach you how to do exactly that, so you won't need me, your best friend, or an expensive resume writer to do it for you.

First, it's necessary to call out the primary goal of a resume, which is to get the interview. Your resume is what gets you in the door, but the main objective is, after they interview you, *not* hiring you shouldn't be an option. The only barrier between you and a company knowing how amazing you are is this piece of paper. That's why our first task is to put your very best attributes and accomplishments on that page, along with your unique skill sets, achievements, and superpowers. This is the time to showcase exactly what you bring to the table, and why you're awesome.

Before you can even begin to approach your resume, though, some important reframing needs to happen. Typically, most of us think a resume should just list our work history and education; this is incorrect. What your resume *actually* needs to be is a brag sheet! People don't talk about this enough, which is why I'm addressing it here. If you're writing your resume any other way, you're doing yourself a disservice. Let's fix it!

There are three core principles to remember when writing your resume:

- **Be compelling:** Tell your story and own what makes you uniquely powerful.
- **Be clear:** Attach numbers and metrics anywhere that you can. I know this part seems daunting, but it really isn't. (We'll cover this in more detail later.)
- **Take credit:** Now is not the time to share credit with any others with whom you've collaborated; this is *your* resume. It's time to take credit for your hard work and celebrate your achievements—big and small.

If it's been a while since you've edited your resume, it's time to revisit the basics.

## RESUME, YOU STAY!

You need the following seven essential sections on your resume:

1. **Headline:** Be clear, and include your industry and job title (for example, Digital Marketing Analyst and Retail Marketing Expert).

2. **About me:** Be compelling and include one or two sentences that emphasize your specific expertise within your industry. Also, be sure to highlight your years of experience (for example, "I am a Digital Marketing Analyst with five years of experience in the retail space. I craft innovative campaigns, build strategic partnerships, and deliver exceptional results for clients,").

3. **Achievements:** Take credit! Include two to four bullets on what you're most proud of in your career, including schooling, volunteer work, or part-time roles (for example, "Launched SEO campaign that generated 10,000 unique visitors and 200 customers monthly,").

4. **Work experience:** Be clear and use dynamic verbs (led, managed, created, strategized, launched, crafted, and so on) to clarify your level of ownership on projects and tasks. Use these to kick off your work experience bullets with a bang. Again, take credit for your accomplishments. Think about where you started and ended in that role. What impact did you make? Metrics (which we'll expand on shortly) are just an estimate—recruiters won't fact-check you. Do your best to gather data and take credit for your hard work.

5. **Certifications and skills:** Include any relevant software, programs, languages, training, and/or certifications that you have.

6. **Contact:** Include your email address, mobile number, and a clickable LinkedIn URL. If it applies to your industry, link your portfolio, as well.

7. **Education:** If you don't have a formal education, you can skip this. These days, in many industries, it's not a hard-and-fast requirement, which is a step in the right direction, as not everyone has access to it. However, if you do have college or post-grad experience, include the name of your school, as well as your major and minor. Your GPA and year of graduation are completely optional. If you're seeking your first job, include any clubs, volunteer work, or extracurricular activities (you can include any from high school, as well.)

## SASHAY AWAY.

You can remove any of the following from your resume:

- Your photo.
- Your home address.
- An objective statement.
- Additional pages (unless you have over fifteen years of highly relevant work experience, your resume should be one page).
- Old or irrelevant work experience.

The work experience section of your resume is the meatiest, so you want to give it special care. It's also important to note that this section doesn't have to be in chronological order. If your most relevant work experience isn't your most recent, you still want to list it first.

The way in which you kick off each bullet that illustrates your work experience says a lot to a recruiter. As someone who has reviewed thousands of resumes, I've truly seen it all and can tell you that this is a crucial, yet simple, change to make. Open your current resume and take a look at the first word of each bullet point under your work experience. Use the following words sparingly and only in cases where they truly apply: coordinated, facilitated, organized, conducted, acted, assisted, provided, and helped. Too often, we use words like these because we're shying away from taking the credit we actually deserve. You might prefer a teamwork mentality and sharing credit where it's due, but again, your resume is not the place for this.

This is where the transformation begins. Fight the urge to give credit to the team. Try to change all of those words to more dynamic verbs, such as: managed, led, crafted, strategized, developed, spearheaded, owned, created, oversaw, and launched.

Dynamic verbs convey a sense of ownership, so when you have a choice between one of the latter or a passive verb, you now know which to choose. By the way, you don't need to have "manager" in your job title to have ownership of tasks and processes. Recruiters just want to see that you were engaged. If you overuse weak verbs, it tells a much less powerful story. You want your resume to pack a powerful punch. It should be a bold, brassy eleven o'clock number sung by one of the great divas, not a meek, barely audible sigh.

Now that we have our dynamic verbs squared away, it's time to dive into metrics. One of the most common resume mistakes I see is job responsibilities listed in the work experience section. Your work experience shouldn't be a list of the responsibilities of that job, but rather, it should be a short list of what you *achieved* at that job, quantified with metrics.

I know this can seem daunting, but here's the secret not enough people are talking about: metrics are a guesstimate. Your company won't provide them for you, so you have to think about where you started in a job versus where you ended. Then, perform a good old-fashioned, as-accurate-as-possible guesstimate because, the truth is, that's what we're all doing on our resumes. Here's an example of a work experience bullet before metrics have been applied:

• Provided exceptional customer service.

There are a few things wrong here. First, we have the weak verb "provided," which isn't doing this person any favors in the ownership department. If you've ever worked a day in customer service, you know what you did went well beyond "providing" anything. Additionally, there are zero metrics or achievements associated with this bullet, but that's not because they don't exist—they absolutely do—we just need to find and articulate them. Writing metrics for your resume is a lot like being a very detail-oriented (and fabulous) detective. You have to dig deep (sometimes, into your memory) and pull out all the information, even if it seems mundane. That's the stuff we're looking for—the finer details. This is where metrics are born.

Here's an example of this same work experience bullet after metrics have been applied:

• Delivered industry-leading customer service and solved 75 cases per day: 40 percent higher than company average, 20 percent of which were escalated cases; increased hotel guest "likely to return" rate by 30 percent.

Now, *this* is what we want to see. Do the metrics have to be exact down to the last decimal? Nope. Should it tell a clear story

## UNDERUSED POWER MOVE

**Resume Personality**

No one tells you this, but your resume should be a reflection of you. Are you a designer? Use more visual elements to illustrate that. Are you a spreadsheet person? Incorporate that into your design. I also include my pronouns and favorite color palette to better convey my personality.

about your impact and achievements? Yes! What you're doing here is smacking them in the face (metaphorically speaking) with exactly why you're perfect for this role. You're showing that you've already achieved everything they need you to do, and more, and that you did all of those things extremely well. These details paint a very clear picture for a recruiter or hiring manager. Essentially, they say, "You've found me! Your search is over."

I sometimes hear, "I don't have any metrics or achievements from my jobs. What should I do?" If you're thinking this, let me dispel that myth for you right now. If you've had (or have) a job of any kind, you have achievements and metrics, you just don't consider them to be those things. That's where you need to shift your perspective and allow your confidence to kick in. It doesn't matter if your job was filing paperwork for eight hours each day, there's still a powerful way to tell that story.

Here's how *not* to write the work experience bullet for that filing job:

- Filed paperwork.

Yeah, this one is in dire need of a full makeover. Here's what it looks like after a day at the spa:

- Managed employee information database and maintained 100 percent compliance for all six audits from 2021–2022.

This revamped, rejuvenated bullet tells the story in fine detail, celebrates the work, and takes ownership of the task. It also illustrates achievement within a clear timeline. Remember, *be clear and compelling, and take credit.* You spent time working there and making an impact, but why? It could've been for many reasons: money, career goals, to try something new, or just to do work you enjoy. The best way to think of all of your work experience is as top-notch content for your badass resume.

But what if there was a period of time when you weren't working at all? One of my most frequently asked resume questions is, "Is it okay to have gaps, and how do I explain them to recruiters?" I'm delighted to tell you that resume gaps are normal: I have them, you have them, we *all* have them.

Below are some of the most common reasons why you might have a gap on your resume:

- You took time off for your mental or physical health.
- You were on parental leave.
- You were raising your family.
- You were taking care of a relative or friend in need.
- You were pursuing a hobby or business venture.
- You were traveling.
- You were between jobs.

All of these (and many more I didn't list) are valid. Some folks like to include the reason for a gap on their resume. For example, on mine, I have a two-month mental health break listed right there between my office jobs. It's totally up to you whether you want to disclose the reason for a gap.

If a recruiter or hiring manager asks you about a gap, the best response is to simply be honest and brief, like any of the following examples:

- "I was taking a necessary mental health break."
- "I was raising my family."
- "I was between jobs, reflecting, and looking for the right fit."
- "I was traveling."
- "I was preparing for a career change."
- "I was taking care of a sick family member."

Any company worth working for will understand any of the reasons above. Again, these pauses are completely normal and, in fact, it's normal to have several of them. Recruiters and hiring managers expect to see gaps, as we all (hopefully) have busy and fulfilling lives outside of work. Rather than "gaps" I consider them to be "meaningful life chapters," and, as a recruiter, I would never hold them against someone. After all, those chapters have helped make you who you are, and that's certainly nothing to apologize for or be ashamed of. I'm proud of the mental health breaks on my resume. If an employer didn't want to hire me because of that, then I certainly don't want to work there.

## COVER LETTER ESP: ELABORATE, SPECIFY, PARALLEL

It's time to address the dreaded cover letter. Sometimes companies ask for them, and sometimes they don't. Sometimes, they don't even read them. Nevertheless, it's important to have a real standout in your back pocket. A cover letter gives you the opportunity to elaborate on your story, and why you're the perfect fit for that role. For career-changers, this is especially important because it allows you to make meaningful connections between your existing skills and a position in a completely new field.

I have a cover letter formula that is incredibly effective and addresses exactly this. Before we dive into that, though, here are some cover letter basics to keep in mind:

- Personalize your letter to suit the job to which you're applying.
- Address your letter to the hiring manager.
- Never rehash your resume.
- Connect the dots for the person who'll be reading it. It should leave them with zero doubt that you're a great fit for the role.
- Keep it to three short paragraphs.

Now, let's demystify how to format a cover letter, once and for all. Follow these steps to conjure a letter that's simple, but still speaks volumes:

1. **Intro:** "Dear (hiring manager's name),".
2. **Elaborate:** Explain precisely why this role is exciting to you and quote the job description.
3. **Specify:** Include two specific examples of why you're a great fit based on your related work experience and metrics.
4. **Parallel:** Connect the dots between your values and those of the company. Mention what you're genuinely passionate about, and how that aligns with the organization.
5. **Sign off:** Say thank you and close with confidence.

Including your metrics is important, and you can easily grab them from your resume. Never apologize for any lack of experience. Instead, focus on the experience you *do* have, as well as your related skills and accomplishments. The truth is, what a recruiter or hiring manager is looking for is unapologetic confidence; that is what really makes us think, "Yes, finally! Here's my hire," so try it on!

When I read a cover letter that's been confidently written, that also highlights a candidate's skills and achievements, in addition to how they're going to jump in and solve a problem, I can't get them on Zoom fast enough.

Let's look at an example of a stellar cover letter that utilizes the ESP method:

*Hello, Natalie,*

*I'm a training and development leader with ten years of experience in the retail space. I'm thrilled to apply for the VP of Training role at Company X. My experience developing training strategy and programs, leading cross-functional training teams, and building Learning Management Systems aligns perfectly with this opportunity and will strongly benefit the team.*

*I'm incredibly passionate about people and equipping them with learning tools that are dynamic and user-friendly. I build enthusiastic teams that put people first, always. This role gets me pumped, as it revolves around what I love to do. (**Elaborate.**)*

*I know you're seeking someone who is a builder, and that's what I do best. I've built industry-leading training teams and global-training strategies from the ground up. In my current role, I created and launched six new full-time training roles, increased training completion rates by 75 percent company-wide, and partnered with Lessonly to build out a brand-new LMS. (**Specify.**)*

*The mission and values of Company X are super aligned with my own, and that excites me! As a sustainable shopper, your brand proposition and execution are inspiring. I own (and swear by) many of your reusable bags. Company X has such an exciting future, and I would be thrilled to be part of shaping it.* (**Parallel.**)

*I would love to bring my wealth of experience and abundant passion for training to Company X. Thank you, and I look forward to continuing the conversation.*

*Best,*
*Sam DeMase*

If you're unsure of the hiring manager's name, you can simply write, "Hello, Hiring Manager at Company X," or try looking them up on LinkedIn. Your final sentence needs to be powerful. You want to drive home the confidence you've weaved throughout your entire letter.

I like to end with, "Thank you, and I look forward to continuing the conversation." This plants the seed that the dialogue between the two of you is just beginning, and that there's much more to discuss during your interview.

## RECRUITER SECRET

Many people use their cover letter as an opportunity to express why they can't wait to join that organization. While there is value in that, it's not the main purpose of a cover letter. What recruiters really want to hear is what exactly you can bring to the table in that role.

## COVER LETTERS FOR CAREER CHANGERS

If you're changing careers, your cover letter is an opportunity to connect your existing skills and experience with a new role. Specify why you're a great fit, but do call out the elephant in the room: that your career history is in a different field, but explain how it's perfectly led you to this new role. Do *not* apologize for any missing work experience. Remember, if you have transferable superpowers, your value goes *up* when you change careers, not down. You'll be bringing unique skills to the team that they don't currently have. You could frame it this way:

> *My five years of experience as a high school English teacher has equipped me extremely well for this learning and development role for the following reasons: . . .*

Then, share examples from your work experience that clearly articulate your story and the value those experiences will bring to this position. Explain why your unique perspective is necessary for the role. You don't want to leave a hiring manager curious as to why you've applied. You want your story to be crystal clear and your examples to be relatable and impactful. Typically, a human does read your cover letter, so leave no doubt in their mind that you're the person they've been looking for.

## STRATEGIC OUTREACH: TWO WAYS

If you're reading this book, you're probably the type of person who doesn't mind a little extra credit every now and then. You have a bomb resume and a powerful-AF cover letter. If you want to sweeten the odds of landing an interview even more, there are two ways you might be able to do it. If it's a job you really want, a company you've admired forever, or you already know someone who works there, it's time for some strategic outreach.

## NICHE NETWORKING

Niche networking is a twist on basic networking that utilizes an important angle. If you really want to work somewhere and you've already applied for a job there, try reaching out to someone who works there with whom you share common ground.

For example, if you're a woman, reach out to another woman on the team you want to join. If you're a woman of color, reach out to a fellow woman of color who already works there. If you're LGBTQ+, reach out to someone who's also LGBTQ+ and either works on that specific team or at the organization.

Folks are more likely to support someone with whom they can identify, as opposed to a random cold note without any context.

Here's how to frame your niche networking LinkedIn message if you're a woman contacting another woman at the company:

*Hello, (name of contact),*

*I've recently applied for the open Marketing Manager position on your team. I'd love to know more about what it's like for women working at Company Z. How do you find the experience? Any wins and challenges you wouldn't mind sharing? I would truly appreciate any thoughts or experiences you could share via LinkedIn or a quick phone chat.*

*Thanks!*
*[Your name]*

You're not asking for a job; you're simply asking someone to share their experience. People are much more willing to discuss this than you might think—especially in today's all-too-common environment of gender inequity in the workplace. But what do you get out of this interaction?

First, if you make a great impression (which you will), they'll remember you. They might even pass your name along to the hiring manager. Then, after you're hired, you'll already have a connection with someone on the team.

Second, you might learn something about the company that you wouldn't have otherwise. Their description of what it's like to work there will speak volumes. It's invaluable intel for you to have and can definitely help inform your decision about whether you want to work there.

## THE VALUE PROPOSITION

This method of strategic networking entails articulating your value, and is just like the **specify** portion of your cover letter. To implement this method of networking, you'll first have to find the hiring manager or someone on the recruiting team at the company where you've applied (start with a LinkedIn search). Then, send them a message similar to the following example to pique their interest:

*Hello, Rosa,*

*I'm a training and development leader with ten years of experience in the retail space. I've recently applied for the VP of Training role at Company X. I know you're seeking someone who is a builder, and that is what I do best!*

*I've built industry-leading training teams and global-training strategies from the ground up. In my current role, I created and launched six new full-time training roles, increased training completion rates by 75 percent company-wide, and partnered with Wisetail to build out a brand-new LMS.*

*The mission and values of Company X are super aligned with my own, and that excites me! As a sustainable shopper, your brand proposition and execution are inspiring. In fact, I own (and swear by) many of your reusable bags. Company X has such an exciting future, and I would be thrilled to be a part of shaping that.*

*Best,*
*[Name]*
*[Email address]*

Sending a message like the above alerts them not only to your recent application, but also to how your skills are going to be immediately impactful on their team. It's also quite low risk with a potentially high reward to send out these kinds of messages. You don't have anything to lose, so why not shoot your shot? You can also combine both strategic outreach methods if you want.

If you happen to know someone at a company where you've applied—even a friend of a friend—ask them to put in a good word for you. On LinkedIn, you can actually see everyone those in your network are connected to, so if you see a possible way in, use it to your advantage.

Every single time a friend has asked me to refer them for a position, I've said yes and done so. Remember, you're not burdening your friends—they want to uplift and help you, so *always* ask your

**1 POWER MEMO** Never be the one to say no to yourself; let them do it, and then you'll be pleasantly surprised (or knowingly pleased) when they say yes!

friends, family, and community for support. Why go it alone? We're all stronger as a collective.

It's also important to consider the big picture and your personal brand. Recruiters and potential employers will often Google you, and check out your social media, so make sure your Twitter, Instagram, and any other accounts you have are looking good.

Think about what your personal brand says about you. Perhaps it proclaims your love of traveling, family, going to concerts, gardening, or whatever else you're into. Always keep in mind that your social media offers a glimpse into who you are, so make sure you're happy with it. Prospective employers will also look at your LinkedIn, so be sure it's completely updated and includes your most recent work experience and skills.

Hopefully, now that you're armed with these tools, you'll apply for the jobs you want, even if you don't meet all of the requirements. All of those who have gotten their dream jobs never let that stop them! Own your work experience and be confident.

I'm not really one for sports metaphors, but I believe someone once said that you miss 100 percent of the shots you don't take, so always shoot your shot!

# CHAPTER 4
## CRUSHING THE INTERVIEW

**POWER MOOD MUSIC**

ABOUT DAMN TIME
BY LIZZO

0:48                        −3:11

In addition to your killer resume, you, of course, need interview confidence. You need moxie, and to build up that sort of fearless self-assurance, you have to be prepared for what's coming. And that's why I'm here to share this *E! True Hollywood Story: The Untold Secrets of Extraordinary Interviewing!*

Like touting our achievements on our resumes, something else we're not taught is how to be exceptional at interviewing. There are many folks out there who have a phenomenal resume, but don't necessarily know how to "play the game" of interviewing, and that isn't fair.

That's why, until things change, I'm here to spill the tea that will help you all infiltrate the system. One day, we'll be able to dismantle this thing from the inside, but for now, we play the game and utilize every single tool we have to our advantage.

To get started, think about the interview question that scares you the most—yes, that one. By the end of this chapter, your fear will be completely assuaged, and that's a promise!

If an interview ever feels like an interrogation, that's a red flag. They should always be conversational because—and never forget this—you're also interviewing them. The process of successful interviewing can be broken down into three parts. If I were to rank them in order of importance, they would be: the prep, the interview conversation, and the follow-up.

Like most other things in life, the key to success lies in the preparation because that is what breeds confidence. There's no better feeling than being expertly prepared for an interview—plus, it essentially guarantees your success. If you've prepared, the odds are extremely high that you'll leave an interview thinking, "Wow! I slayed that!"

**2 | POWER MEMO** An interview is a conversation, **not** an interrogation.

## THE PREP

Once again, you could have the greatest resume of all time, but you also need to be able to clearly articulate your value during the interview. Trust me, the hiring manager *wants* to fill that role with the right person. If you're visibly and audibly confident and well-spoken during the interview, that's a big piece of the puzzle. When you're confident in your skills, they can be confident (and excited!) to move you forward to the next step.

Your goal is not only to make it easy for them to do that, but also to make it *impossible* for them not to. Make it difficult for the interviewer not to compliment you right there on the first call. I've done it many times, so a lot of y'all are succeeding! You can be the unicorn, it's all about how you sell it.

So, how exactly do you prep for an interview? Follow these four steps:

1. **Research the people:** Once you have the names of your interviewers, look them up on LinkedIn, and then head to Google. Do some digging, and see if you can find any common ground the two of you might share. For example, maybe you're both from the same area, previously worked at the same company, have a mutual friend, etc. People love talking about themselves, so if you can weave a personal nugget that you know about them into the conversation, they'll be impressed.

2. **Review the company's mission and values:** Similar to the parallel in your cover letter, think about where you and this company align. Maybe you've purchased and loved their products, or you admire the community work they do or appreciate how they take care of their employees. You can usually find all of this information on the company's website, so look for sections on the menu or header that refer to the organization's mission, values, team, and culture.

3. **Learn what's new and noteworthy:** Do a search on the company via Google *and* Google News so you can see their most recent headlines. It's important to be current on things like their new product launches, initial public offerings (IPOs), leadership announcements, and Diversity, Equity, and Inclusion goals. Then, you can reference these in your conversation to show that you

## RECRUITER SECRET

As someone with extensive recruiting and hiring experience, I can tell you that we all **want** you to succeed. There's nothing we love more than speaking with someone who exudes confidence, and has obviously done their research on the company and the role. That is the unicorn we've been waiting for!

have your finger on the pulse of what this company is doing. Sometimes, interviewers will refer to current happenings, and you definitely don't want to be caught off guard.

4. **Prepare examples:** This is the most pivotal part of the prep phase because it's precisely what can turn an interview from "meh," to "wow!" and secure you the job. Specific examples are important because they play right into the interviewer's goal of finding someone who can solve their problem. If you provide specific examples of how you've solved similar problems successfully, it removes all the guesswork for them and allows them to feel incredibly confident about you. They won't want to let you go, and you'll also have some major leverage when it comes to salary negotiation. Hence, preparing well for the interview will drive up your value (which we love!).

That all sounds super easy, right? But wait—how do you prepare the right examples? Well, first, you have to know (and understand) some of the different types of interview questions you might be asked.

## THE FOUR TYPES OF INTERVIEW QUESTIONS

To crush the interview, it helps to have an idea of what you're walking into. Something you'll notice quite quickly as you go on more job interviews is that all recruiters and hiring managers tend to ask the same questions. This is excellent because it allows you to practice!

Below are four of the most common types of interview questions and some examples of each:

1. **Skill-based:** As you probably guessed, these types of questions are all about your skills and certifications. For example, you might be asked, "How proficient are you in X software?" Remember to always be confident in your abilities and avoid underselling yourself. Think you're "average" when it comes to a a certain software? Upgrade that to "highly proficient" (you can always brush up before you start the job).

2. **Situational:** These future-focused questions relate specifically to the job, such as, "How would you handle X situation with a client?" Search for examples of these and prepare some responses.

3. **Personality:** These are the fun questions because they're all about who you are. I love when companies ask these questions because it shows they care about more than just solving a problem—they also care about who you are. It's also a good indication that they embrace bringing your "whole self" to work, which is key. Examples of some personality questions might include:

   - "How would you describe yourself in three words?"
   - "What's your favorite restaurant?"
   - "Is there a podcast, book, or movie that you recommend?"

4. **Behavioral:** These are the most commonly asked and toughest interview questions to get right—if you're unprepared, that is. These are the inquiries about your previous work experience. Typically, they're framed something like, "Tell me about a time when (insert challenging work situation here)." These questions can really cause some flop sweat if you haven't properly prepped. Luckily, I have a formula for answering these questions that delivers every single time (more on that later).

Once you know you have an interview coming up, it's time to search the internet for the questions candidates are most commonly asked within your industry. For example, if you're in marketing, you might search, "behavioral interview questions for brand manager interview." This should return a bunch of example questions for that role. Use any prompts that you find to build your responses in a digital document. This way, your answers will be available for a quick review whenever you need them.

Some examples of frequently asked behavioral questions include:

- What is your biggest strength?
- What is your biggest weakness?
- Has there ever been a time when you disagreed with your leader? Tell me about it.
- Can you describe a time when you made a mistake at work, and how you handled it?

Before you start sweating, I'm about to introduce you to my proprietary method for answering behavioral questions with a level of finesse that'll leave the interviewer stunned (in a good way).

## THE CARE METHOD FOR ANSWERING BEHAVIORAL INTERVIEW QUESTIONS

If you've been researching job interview tips and tricks, you've most likely come across the STAR method. This acronym stands for Situation, Task, Action, Result, and it's a popular shortcut to help you remember how to answer behavioral interview questions. There's nothing wrong with the STAR method; however, I thought it was missing some important elements interviewers tend to be looking for, and that's why I created the CARE method:

- **Context:** A brief explanation of the circumstances.
- **Action:** The action you took.
- **Result:** The results of the action you took.
- **Evolution:** How you grew and evolved as a result of this situation (this part is the frequently forgotten cherry on top).

When you prepare for an interview using the CARE method, it's a real game changer because it takes the guesswork, nervousness, and fear out of answering these types of questions. Preparing stellar, specific examples for answering behavioral questions is important because it enables you to provide your interviewer with concrete proof of your abilities, excellence, and unique talents. You won't have to resort to giving some half-hearted, vague answer. Instead, you'll be able to hand over the receipts of your prowess, which will make you feel incredibly powerful in the moment.

Let's look at an example of CARE in action when answering the especially tricky behavioral question, "Can you describe a time when you made a mistake at work?"

While the mistake you choose for your example should absolutely be something that really happened, you don't want to lower your chances of landing the job—you want to increase them. With this in mind, you want to avoid sharing anything directly related to any of the core requirements for the role for which you're interviewing. What the interviewer is looking for here is how you responded to the mistake. Did you recover quickly, and learn from it? Great! That's what they want to hear.

Here's an example of a stellar response:

> *At my last job, I was in charge of a project that involved multiple stakeholders (**Context**), and I accidentally sent an important email to the wrong person (**Action**). As a result, there was a brief delay in the project timeline. I owned up to it, corrected my mistake, and we quickly got back on track (**Result**). I tend to be a big-picture thinker, so this taught me a lot about the importance of honing in on the fine details. At the time, I was hard on myself, but now I realize that, moving forward, this made me a much more detail-oriented project manager (**Evolution**).*

You can see why the evolution part is so important: it places less focus on the mistake and more on what you learned from it, which is exactly what recruiters want to hear. We all make mistakes at work— I've made several today! It's all about what you take away from it and how it helps you evolve as a person and a professional. This is also storytelling, which is extremely tough to do on the fly. That's why the preparation phase is so important. When you think about these answers ahead of time and thoughtfully prepare your answers and examples, there's no possible outcome other than success.

## LINKING BACK AND A BIT OF INVESTIGATION

Another tip for responding effectively to behavioral questions is to link back to the role for which you're applying. Whenever you get the opportunity, quote the job description back to them. This will inform them that you're the person they're looking for! The "What is your biggest strength?" question is a great moment for you to select one that's also critical to success in that position. Bonus points for calling that out in your response!

For example, you might say something like, "My biggest strength is being a future-focused, visionary leader. In my last role I spearheaded an innovative marketing strategy that led to a 60 percent increase in sales that quarter. I know that in this role, you're seeking someone who's a builder and will challenge the status quo, and that's what I do best."

You'll see from your Google search that there are a lot of different behavioral questions. They run the gamut from your adaptability and communication style, to teamwork and persuasion skills. To hone your answers even more, I highly recommend you check out the interview questions and employee review sections for the company on Glassdoor. Folks often post the questions they were asked during their interviews in both of those places.

You can also reach out to friends (or friends of friends) who have interviewed in that industry or at that company and ask what their experience was like. Any insider info you can get is worth seeking out because it can give you a leg up!

## ANSWERING (ONE OF) THE MOST UNIVERSALLY DESPISED INTERVIEW QUESTIONS

Let's address the first nominee for the "Most Universally Despised Interview Question" award: "Can you tell me a bit about yourself?" This one is annoying because it's so broad. It's also just really lazy, but does it still get asked? Yes.

This question is typically asked at the beginning of an interview to give the hiring manager an idea of who you are, rather than just hearing a rehash of your resume (which they'll hopefully already have in front of them). What they really want is a confident introduction from you. They'll be listening not only to what you say, but also to how you say it. Is it long-winded? Do you sound resigned and tired?

As someone who's hosted approximately a trillion interviews, I was always impressed when a candidate had a concise and confident intro ready. It really starts your interview off on a wonderful high note, like you're serving the recruiter a double shot of metaphorical espresso.

Luckily, I know exactly how to answer this question, and it's easy to prepare. Plus, unlike most of the other interview questions, once you prep this one, you'll have it locked in for every single future interview. My suggested approach for answering this question was one of my very first mega-viral videos on TikTok (it now has 15+ million views). I call it the WAT Method, and it goes a little something like this:

- **What you do:** This is your headline.
- **Achievements:** What you've achieved in the past that most relates to this role. You can pull these from the Specify section of your cover letter.
- **Tie-in:** Talk about the specific role, and why you're excited about it. Like the above, you can pull these from the Elaborate section of your resume. Why do more work when you don't have to?

Here's an example of how you might use WAT to answer the "tell me about yourself" question:

> *I'm a training and development leader with over ten years of experience in the hospitality space (**W**). I've built strategy from the ground up, created and launched seven new training roles, and increased overall training completions globally by 50 percent in my current role (**A**). I'm pumped about this role because, not only am I ready for this next challenge, but I'm also very passionate about the work you do in the sustainability space (**T**).*

This brief, but powerful, three-sentence intro packs quite a punch. You might also want to pepper in a bit about your personal hobbies, interests, passions, side hustles, and so on, after the Tie-in. For example, you could add that you love musicals, baking, playing video games, and that you also raise horses in your spare time. (That's quite an interesting person I made up—are you really out there?)

When you use the WAT method at the start of an interview, you accomplish three critical things right away:

1. **You emanate confidence:** Part of interviewing successfully involves your ability to clearly articulate your value, and the WAT method provides you with a strong way to do that from the start. Your response will show that you're excited about this opportunity, because you cared enough to prepare a compelling intro.

2. **You exude competence:** Again, right off the bat, you're answering one of the most important questions every interviewer has: does this person achieve results? Your Achievements will prove that you not only have the qualifications, you brought the receipts! This will confirm that you're their unicorn.

3. **You foster conversation:** By citing specific examples from your work experience, you give the interviewer something tangible to use as a jumping off point for their next question. You'll immediately allow them to see you in the role, which is key.

## THE DREADED SALARY QUESTION

When it comes to the most feared (and hated) interview questions, nothing beats: "What are your salary expectations?" Like "tell me about yourself," this one can trigger nervousness, stress, and panic faster than any of the other interview questions combined. However, that's why we prepare, right?

I have two top-tier ways to answer the salary question, depending on the situation:

- **Early in the process:** "Since we're still early in the interview process, I don't yet have a handle on the full scope of what this role entails. Can you share the salary range?"
- **If they don't provide a range or later in the process:** "Based on my experience, accomplishments, and the current market rate, I'm looking for something in the range of $X–Y. Is that within your range for this role?"

## THE FEARLESS CAREERIST
### KNOW YOUR WORTH, PLUS TAX!

When you provide a salary range, you want to make sure the amount you actually want (your magic number) is at the bottom of that range. For example, if you're aiming for 90K, you would give a range of something like 90–110K. We'll delve more deeply into how you find your magic number in the next chapter, but this approach will help you avoid undervaluing yourself and ensure that you're paid fairly.

These responses are both confident and collaborative. I recommend you commit them to memory, or store them digitally so you'll always have them in your back pocket. The first one is great to use when it's early on in the interview process. If they refuse to give you a range (ugh!), then you can move on to option two and share yours—even if they won't be transparent, it's in your best interest to do so. This way, if the salary is below your requirements, you won't have to waste any more of your time.

Even if they never provide a salary range, you'll know based on their response if your number falls within it. We'll cover how to figure out what your salary range is and how to avoid undercutting yourself in the next chapter.

## THE INTERVIEW CONVERSATION

A super common question I often get about interviews is, "What should I do if I don't know the answer or completely blank out?" This is why preparation is so key, but hey, this can happen to even the most prepared among us. You have three choices in this scenario, and all of them are good:

1. **Bend their question to suit one of your prepared examples.** You could say something like, "I was in a similar situation once, and here's how I handled x, y, and z."
2. **Describe what you *would* do.** If you don't have any firsthand experience that applies, describe what you would do if you found yourself in that particular scenario.
3. **Say that you look forward to expanding your experience.** If a question completely stumps you, there's absolutely nothing wrong with being honest about that. Just express that you have a desire to learn. Say something like, "I don't have any direct experience with that, but that's why I'm so excited about this role. I really want to expand my expertise."

## UNDERUSED POWER MOVE

### Always Use an Interview as a Platform

Approach every interview as if you know you're their ideal candidate and the interview is merely an opportunity for you to provide factual evidence of this. Respond to each question strategically, so that you're always sharing your achievements. This will ensure you leave the meeting confident that you've provided your evidence and with zero regrets!

If you find yourself blanking out and need to buy some time, you can always say something like, "Let me think about that for a second. I want to give you a thoughtful response," or, "I'd like to reflect on that. Can we come back to that question in a bit?" We're all human, after all, and none of us is perfect.

When it comes to asking questions during an interview, remember, it's a conversation, not an interrogation. The best way to approach questions is to weave them in organically throughout the interview. Once you get used to doing this, you'll never go back to the old way. The conversational approach to an interview is ideal for both parties. Plus, it gives you the opportunity to interview *them*, as well.

Odds are you won't get to ask all of your questions, but it's good to save some for the end because they'll typically ask, "What other questions do you have for me?"

Keep in mind that the interviewer is paying attention to the questions you do and don't ask. If you don't have *anything* to ask, it's not a great look. You want to exhibit curiosity and interest in the nuances of the role. More importantly, asking questions is an excellent way to determine if you actually want the job! It should always be a two-way street.

If you're unsure what to ask, there are two types of questions: role-specific and company-specific. Role-specific questions signal to the interviewer that you're prepared and ready to take on the job. Folks who don't ask any role-specific questions run the risk of being viewed as unprepared.

Furthermore, you do yourself a disservice if you don't dive deeper into the nuances of a role. To figure out if you're really excited about a gig or not, you need to gather information. The more information you obtain, the easier it'll be for you to make an informed decision.

Below are some examples of excellent role-specific questions you might want to ask:

- How is success defined and measured in this role?
- What are the top goals this person should accomplish within the first three months?
- What are the biggest challenges this person will face?
- What is the onboarding and training process like for this role?
- What professional development opportunities are available in this role?
- Why is this role vacant?
- What roles have others moved on to from here?

Some awesome company-specific questions you might want to ask include:

- How has the company pivoted during COVID-19?
- Do you have a Diversity, Equity, and Inclusion team? What initiatives have they launched recently?
- What do you love most about working here?
- How have you evolved since joining the team here?
- What's next for the company?
- What gets you excited about the future?
- How does the company help its employees maintain a healthy work-life balance?

Jot down some notes when they respond because these might prompt additional questions from you. Just let it unfold organically and see where the conversation goes. You might also have some more general questions that wouldn't necessarily apply to you if you were working in that specific role. For example, you might want to know more details about the structure of the team, leadership, if there is a flexible work policy, and so on.

Whatever is important to you about a job or the company you work for, now's the time to ask. It's best to ask all questions upfront so you can make an informed decision later. If you don't get the chance to ask everything in the initial interview (or if more questions come up later), be sure to ask them in future interview rounds or via email.

Of course, you can also ask questions after you receive an offer, but we'll cover that in more detail in the next chapter.

## PRO TIPS TO CRUSH THE INTERVIEW

If you followed all of the prepping tips and have practiced your answers to the four types of interview questions you're likely to be asked, you're already in pretty good shape! Below are a few more tips worth keeping in mind that will help you nail that interview:

- **Use psychology to your advantage:** Always use the interviewer's name when you greet them. When people hear their name spoken out loud, it makes them feel seen. Employ reflective listening by repeating what they say. This shows that you have a grasp on what they need. At the end of the interview, say, "Thanks. I'm looking forward to continuing the conversation!" This firmly plants the seed in their mind that the dialogue is far from over.
- **Speak slowly:** If you tend to be a naturally fast talker like me (hi, NYC peeps!), you'll need to consciously slow down your tempo during an interview. Speaking fast comes across as nervous and unsure, while slower speech conveys thoughtfulness, confidence, and self-assuredness. Check out

some of Michelle Obama's speeches on YouTube. She speaks slowly and with intention, so every word she says carries weight. If you struggle with this, stage a mock interview with a friend to practice or record yourself speaking.

- **Ask questions throughout the interview:** We covered this in the previous section, but it bears repeating: an interview is a conversation, not an interrogation. The best way to keep a conversation flowing is to ask questions as they come up.
- **Don't absorb the interviewer's potential lack of energy:** If the interviewer doesn't have the energy or personality you were hoping for, don't let it immediately bring you down. Often, your first interview at a company will be with a recruiter, and you might be the fortieth person they've spoken to that day. This only becomes a red flag if every single person you meet at an organization displays the same type of detached energy.
- **Be your true self:** I saved the most important tip for last: bring your whole self to the interview. Allow your personality, essence, and vibe to shine through. You want to work somewhere that encourages you to be you, so test that out right away. If you're funny, let it out! If you're an intellectual, rock it. And if you're more on the quiet side, that's great, too—every company needs thoughtful people like you.

## PRO TIPS TO CRUSH A VIRTUAL INTERVIEW

A lot of interviews are virtual these days, and I also have some helpful tips for those that will set you up for success. If you're being interviewed virtually on Zoom, Google Meet, or any other video-chat program, these tips will help you crush it:

- **Test your technology and lighting beforehand:** Make sure your internet connection, computer, webcam, and microphone are all functioning properly. Check how you appear on-camera, and make sure you're well-lit. If possible, try to have a light source in front of you.

- **Organize your space and background:** It's best to have a clean, uncluttered space behind you so the focus will be on you. Many video-chat programs also have backgrounds available, so use one of those if it would look better.
- **Pour yourself a glass of water:** If your throat gets too dry, or you feel a tickle mid-interview, you'll be glad it's there.
- **Have a clean notepad (digital or analog) in front of you:** This way you can easily jot down any notes or questions that come to mind.
- **Have your resume and CARE-prepared responses in front of you:** These can be on your computer or a piece of paper, but just make sure they're there so you can quickly reference them.
- **Strike a power pose and play your favorite song right before:** This can instantly boost your mood and ensure you're standing in your power.

## RED AND GREEN FLAGS

No one wants to work for a company that treats its employees poorly, burns them out, and/or discards them often. That's why it's important to be on the lookout for any red flags during a job interview.

Contrary to popular belief, there *are* good companies to work for out there, you just have to learn how to listen to your gut because it's almost always right. This is especially important if you're already trying to leave a toxic workplace—you don't want to jump from one bad situation right into another.

They're not always this obvious, but here are some of the most common red flags that could come up during an interview:

- The interviewer is unprepared, disinterested, and/or disrespectful.
- They ask you illegal, invasive personal questions related to your gender, religion, sexual orientation, disability, marital status, pregnancy, and so on.

# THE FEARLESS CAREERIST
## SHUTTING DOWN ILLEGAL INTERVIEW QUESTIONS

Any question that makes you feel even slightly uncomfortable during a job interview is a red flag, but the following are definitely no-go's:

- Do you plan on getting pregnant any time soon?
- Are you married?
- Do you have any children?
- How old are you?
- Are you religious?

If you're ever asked any of the above, a good way to respond is, "May I ask how this relates to the job responsibilities?" This will signal to the interviewer that you know the question was inappropriate. Depending on the severity, you might also want to alert the company's human resources department and/or your local labor board afterward.

- Everyone you meet seems disorganized, unhappy, or burnt out.
- They don't give you any time to ask questions and/or struggle to answer yours.
- There seems to be a lot of confusion about the role and its responsibilities.
- They mention that employee morale is low.
- They say they don't allow salary negotiation.

We hear about red flags all the time, but are there any positive signs you should note during an interview? Indeed, there are green flags too, they just aren't talked about nearly enough.

Below are some excellent signs that the company you've applied to has a healthy work environment:

- Everyone you interview with speaks highly of the company culture and professional development opportunities.
- The role you're interviewing for is vacant because someone got promoted.
- The interview process is organized and efficient.
- They answer all of your questions in detail.
- You genuinely enjoy the conversations you have with each interviewer.
- They're transparent about the salary and benefits.

It's pretty much standard procedure nowadays, but if you make it to the final round of interviewing and haven't yet spoken with someone on the actual team you'd be working with, request to do so. This will give you a lot of insight into what it's like to work there, the boss's leadership style, and the company's culture.

Plus, it will show them that you're invested in the process—it's a win-win! You'll get to have a meaningful, clarifying conversation, and they'll know that you're enthusiastic about joining the team.

## THE THANK-YOU AND FOLLOW-UP

It's important to send a thank-you note after every job interview you have, but the good news is you don't have to think too hard about these. The single biggest mistake folks tend to make is either not sending one at all, or saying something super generic and bland, like "Thank you for your time. I look forward to hearing from you." That is not memorable at all.

What we're looking for is a note from the person we enjoyed speaking with. Keep it brief, but make it memorable by mentioning specific things you discussed during your conversation. They'll absolutely appreciate it, and it'll cement you for that second- or third-round interview.

I've taken all guesswork out of it for you—these vital tips will help you compose a memorable thank-you email:

- Send it within twenty-four hours (or sooner!). The end of the day on which you were interviewed is ideal. Then, it will be one of the first messages they see in their inbox the next morning.
- Keep it short and sweet.
- Actually say "thank you," but try to personalize it so it's not the same as everyone else's.
- Quote something the interviewer said that excited you about the role.
- Highlight once again how your job experience relates directly to the role.
- Close with excitement about speaking to them again soon.

Let's take a look at a sparkling example of a post-interview thank-you email:

*Hi, Mariah,*

*Thanks so much for connecting with me today. It's always a joy to chat with a fellow RPDR fan! I really enjoyed our conversation and hearing about [company name], where things are currently, and the exciting challenges facing the Director of L&D role.*

*You mentioned that building out the L&D team is a priority, and team development is not only one of my areas of expertise, it's also one of my passions. I have no doubt that my ten years of experience in L&D in the retail space, along with my zest for exceptional hospitality and stellar culture, would be a great addition to your team.*

*Looking forward to continuing the conversation.*
*Thanks again!*

*Best,*
*[Your Name]*

So, you prepared, did your research, totally crushed the interview, and sent a thank-you email, but it's been a while, and you haven't heard anything. It's time to follow-up! At least twice a day, I hear, "I haven't heard from the company I interviewed with a week ago. Should I follow up?"

The answer is yes! You should *always* follow up. First, though, save your sanity and try not read too much into it when they don't get back to you right away. Companies have a tendency to be at least slightly (or very) disorganized during the hiring process—that's why one that isn't is a *major* green flag.

You might be thinking, *I don't want to be annoying. They're probably just super busy. I'll just wait and see.* This is your inner imposter-syndrome voice, and she's flat-out wrong— ignore her! Following up doesn't come off as annoying; on the contrary, it shows that you're organized, driven, and interested! You're not "bothering" anyone; you're simply reminding them how amazing your interview was and keeping yourself in the forefront of their mind. You'll never not be hired because you followed up, but you certainly might not get hired if you don't (catch my drift?). A candidate that never follows up isn't usually the person who gets the job.

Of course, you do want to strike the right balance when it comes to timing. If you don't hear back from them within the time frame they originally stated, it's time to send your first follow-up email. If you still don't hear anything back, send another email five business days later.

If you're unsure about what to write, here's an example you can use to frame your follow-up email:

> *Hello, Sasha,*
>
> *I really enjoyed chatting with you about the [job title] role and just wanted to check in on the next steps. I look forward to continuing the conversation!*
>
> *Best,*
> *[Your Name]*

When you add interviews with other companies into the mix, it can get a bit more complicated, which is why it's also important that you're transparent about that in your message. However, this should also light a fire under them to get things moving again. In this case, you would want to add a second paragraph similar to the following:

> *I'm currently in the final round of interviews with another company, but remain incredibly excited about the opportunity to work with you. Are there any updates you could provide about the process and timeline?*

 **3** **POWER MEMO** If you don't get the job (what were they thinking?), keep in mind that rejection is protection. That opportunity wasn't meant for you, and that's okay. However, if you enjoyed the interview process and could see yourself working there in the future, definitely respond and let them know.

When you don't get a job you were really excited about, it's understandable to be super bummed, but it's still a good idea to respond to the rejection email. Perhaps they have another role you would be a good fit for, or a new opportunity will open up in the future. Here's an example of a short-and-sweet response to a rejection email that will send you off on the highest note possible:

> *Thank you for the update. While I'm disappointed we won't be working together, I want to thank you once again for your time and the great conversations we had throughout the process. Please do keep me in mind for any future opportunities.*
>
> *Wishing you all the best!*
> *[Your Name]*

I do know people who have gotten job offers down the road from simply sending a note like this. Often, it's because the person the company hires doesn't work out. Guess whose door they tend to come knocking on in their time of need? If you haven't moved on to another fabulous role by then, your going rate will have just gone up *at least* another 20 percent.

Whew! That was a lot, so let's do a quick, in-a-nutshell recap of how to crush that interview:

- Approach every interview as a conversation, not an interrogation.
- Prepare your CARE examples and practice ahead of time.
- Bring your confidence and personality.
- Ask insightful, curious questions both during the interview and at the end.
- Personalize your thank-you email and make it memorable.
- Don't fear the follow-up, own it!

# CHAPTER 5

## NAILING THE NEGOSH

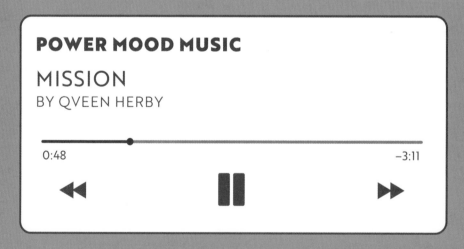

**POWER MOOD MUSIC**

MISSION
BY QVEEN HERBY

0:48                                                   −3:11

Negotiation is the cornerstone of my business and my life. In fact, it's one of the main reasons I started Power Mood in the first place. Years ago, my friends and family started coming to me for salary negotiation advice, but in 2020, I helped a friend specifically regarding what to say, and how to say it.

A few days later, she emailed and told me she'd gotten everything she'd asked for, including a higher salary and more advanced title. Needless to say, we were both thrilled!

The giddy, powerful feeling of advocating for yourself and then getting exactly what you want is contagious!

As we were celebrating, it occurred to me that I needed to share this information with more women so we can all start making the money we deserve. I started Power Mood shortly thereafter, and here we are!

Because money has always been considered a symbol of status and power, most of it has long been held and controlled by men and the broader societal patriarchy. As a result, like many others, while I've always been passionate about women earning what they're worth, I wasn't always inherently confident enough to do so for myself. Several additional factors have contributed to this, as well.

First, when I was growing up, salary negotiation just wasn't a topic my parents ever spoke to me about. In fact, my mom never really talked about money with me at all, let alone how to go about making sure I earned what I was worth. This wasn't her fault, of course. She grew up during an era in which women held significantly less power—financially and otherwise.

She was also raised by my incredibly strong grandma—a single mother who was always overburdened and repeatedly taken advantage of financially. Somehow, though, grandma always strategically shielded my mom from this. It wasn't until I was in my late twenties that my mom finally shared this knowledge with me.

Money is still considered by many to be a taboo topic, and this is especially true among women. There's a lot of shame attached to the previous decades, along with intergenerational trauma. It's even more complex for women of color, who not only carry the latter, but also the burden of systemic racism and white supremacy.

While I had strong, confident female role models in my mom, aunt, and both grandmas (one of whom, I'm lucky enough to still have in my life), advocating for one's self was, again, just not a topic that ever came up. When they discussed their careers, the conversations tended to be along the lines of, "we're so lucky to have jobs at all right now, given the current economic state." Like many of us, I was definitely raised to be confident, but I had no clue about how to ask for my worth. My mom and grandma instilled in me that I was talented, unique, and worthy, but that dialogue never included money.

It was from several other women I later met (both educators) that I first heard about the struggle of low pay and deteriorating mental health, along with the incredibly high level of commitment and results they were expected to deliver. It didn't add up. They were working insanely hard in a highly esteemed profession, and for what? To be severely underpaid, exhausted, and gaslit by their principals? It's not my intent to generalize the experience of all educators and teachers—this was merely what I learned secondhand from those I've known in that profession.

As I started my professional career, I carried all of this with me. While I didn't have an immediate plan or solution, I had an inkling that I wanted my career experience to be different. This took me a minute to suss out. In my early working days, I was a strong advocate for myself in a lot of ways, but not when it came to salary. When I was offered my first job, I didn't negotiate the salary at all, but simply accepted the first offer. I honestly didn't even know negotiating your salary was an option!

Over the following few years, two things happened. First, I began to notice inequities at my workplace. My industry, like so many others, was and still is male dominated. I observed that it was mainly men who were getting promoted by other men and given second, third, fourth, and fifth chances after poor work performance, or even after committing sexual harassment! This was all deeply unsettling.

Second, I started having conversations about salary with my colleagues and friends, which were eye-opening. People were actually starting to talk about gender pay inequity, and you better believe I was listening closely. Because I wasn't raised in an environment in which we talked openly about money, it was refreshing and empowering to finally be able to do so. It was like I was finally being told a huge secret. All of these injustices were happening, but everyone was keeping them quiet.

However, with all of this bubbling under the surface, I knew something was coming. The combination of seeing my employer turn a blind eye to (and eventually, incentivizing) men who were harassing women, and the conversations I was having with female colleagues about salary empowered me. These men were out here being awful *and* making more money than me? It was absolutely criminal! This is when I started actively thinking about my worth and negotiating for it.

Initially, though, I didn't get what I asked for—not even close. For almost three years, I was consistently rejected for the promotion and raise I deserved. I built strong business cases (more on that shortly), talked to my colleagues about salary, and advocated for myself every step of the way. I felt like I was banging on every possible door, only to have them all slammed in my face. My boss repeatedly told me, "Next year will be your time," while simultaneously, dozens of men around me were promoted for their potential. I had a list a mile long of achievements and the impact I'd made on the business and its people, yet still, I was rejected when I asked for some tangible recognition. To this day, it's infuriating!

It was this experience that led me to begin researching statistics on women in leadership. According to a study conducted by Lorman in 2021, women currently represent 47 percent of the workplace. However, in 2020, for every one hundred men promoted to manager, only eighty-five women received that same promotion and, of those, only seventy-one were Latina and fifty-eight were Black women.

At the beginning of 2020, women held 38 percent of all manager-level positions, while men held 62 percent. The Fortune 500 list is comprised of 463 male CEOs, while only thirty-seven are female, and only 4.6 percent of these seats are held by women of color.

Learning all of this while also trying to navigate my own challenging career situation inspired me to start swapping stories with other women and share my own experience more broadly. It was also the impetus of eventually starting my business, which has now helped thousands of other women start making a lot more money and leave toxic jobs. Oh yeah, and it also led me to write this book, so thanks, former employers!

To put this in the proper context, though, it's important to talk about the reality of my situation. I'm a privileged white woman, and this was still considerably tough. For women of color, who face multiple systems of oppression simultaneously, it's much more than tough—it can be a major, and seemingly insurmountable hurdle of injustice.

We need look no further than the gender and race wage gap to, unfortunately, find proof of this. A 2020 report by the U.S. Census Bureau compared the wages of white men to those of white, Black, and Latina women. White women were paid 79 percent, Black women 64 percent, and Latina women 57 percent.

This is precisely why it's so important to talk about money and *not* place the burden of closing the wage gap on women. It's past time to hold companies and society accountable and no longer remain silent about this injustice.

One of the reasons I care so much about negotiation is that it's not taught in schools or even in many peoples' families. It's guarded like some sort of secret for privileged men. It's a powerful, severely underutilized tool that we can use to our advantage to thrive in a system that wasn't built for us. Every single time I negotiate, I do it for those who couldn't: my mom, my aunt, and my grandmas. I do it to raise the bar for the women who'll come after me, and that is what Power Mood is all about.

In 2018, global staffing firm Robert Half conducted a survey and found that only 46 percent of men and 34 percent of women negotiated their salaries.

Those percentages aren't high enough, especially for women. We should *all* be negotiating our salaries for some very important reasons. First, employers expect it; negotiation is a standard part of the hiring process. Generally, it's the company's goal to hire you on as cheaply as possible. *Your* goal, however, is to effectively communicate your value and negotiate for what you're worth. When more of us negotiate, we increase our collective bargaining power, and continue to raise the bar for the women and other marginalized folks who'll follow us.

Before we dive into strategy, I want you to think about how the idea of negotiating something makes you feel. Do you feel nervous or anxious? Terrified or excited? How about a combo of all of those? All feelings are valid, and it can help to explore why the idea of negotiating makes you feel that way. I'm also going to challenge you to think about negotiation in a different way than you ever have before.

One of my favorite negotiation mindsets of all time is to think of negotiation as a *collaboration*, not a *confrontation*; repeat it out loud like a mantra. The more you truly internalize and believe this, the easier (and more fun) your negosh will be. Remember, they want you to work there. You've just been put through a lengthy, tedious interview process. The last thing they want is for you to walk away now, because then, they'll have to start the whole process all over again. They *want* to collaborate with you and meet your needs.

By the end of this chapter, you'll not only know how to expertly prep for a negosh, but you'll also know how to approach the conversation with confidence and power. Additionally, you'll learn exactly what verbiage to use, and—last, but not least—you'll actually be *excited* about negotiating! It's true; you'll not only be more than ready to advocate for what you deserve, you'll be hyped about doing it, and that is an amazing feeling.

Mindset blocks and negative self-talk regarding negotiation are very real, and they're rooted in the patriarchy (surprise!). The system has told women for centuries that we must remain humble, and humble people don't negotiate. It's become ingrained in us that we don't deserve the privilege to negotiate for our worth and, even worse, that we can't handle it. All of this is utter BS. We have to push past this nonsense to get what we deserve.

Below are a few extremely common salary negotiation mindset blocks and my debunking of their nonsense:

- **I don't deserve it:** Yes, you do, but *you* must believe that before you can successfully advocate for yourself. Remember, they *want* you to work there—you're a major catch! So now, they have to collaborate with you to seal the deal.
- **I'm afraid they'll say no:** That is where negotiation begins, so you should expect it to be part of the process.
- **I'm afraid they'll revoke the offer:** This is extremely unlikely. In fact, I've never experienced this, nor has anyone I've worked with. If it does happen, be happy, because you definitely do *not* want to work there. Imagine how any future conversations about pay and raises would have gone.
- **I don't want to appear ungrateful:** What if I told you that you could ask for what you're worth *and* express gratitude in the same sentence? Stay tuned.
- **Negotiation doesn't apply to my industry:** There are other things you can negotiate for, including the job title, a remote or flexible work schedule, paid time off, tuition reimbursement, and more. However, if negotiation of base salary is important to you, then it should also be a key factor in deciding which field you go into.

- **I'm sure the company's struggling due to COVID-19 (or the economy, or the state of the industry, or insert other excuse here):** Every industry has been affected by the pandemic; therefore, it's a level playing field. Most employees have also been asked to do more with less training and support. This means your responsibilities and achievements have also likely increased during this period. I negotiated for a promotion and a raise at the height of the pandemic and got it. Ask for what you're worth—pandemic or not!
- **Their offer seems fair and it's more than I make now:** Just because it's more than you make now doesn't mean it's what you're worth. I don't want you to be paid just a bit more; I want you to be paid what you deserve. So, you need to do your research, find out what that magic number is, and then negotiate for it!
- **I have no idea what to say, or how to go about it:** I gotchu! By the time you've finished this chapter, you'll not only be prepared for your next salary negotiation, you'll be hyped about it!

## THE FEARLESS CAREERIST
### REGRET? WHO'S SHE?

I can't tell you how many times I've heard, "I wish I had negotiated my salary. I just accepted their first offer," or, "They were so excited when I accepted. I bet they would've gone higher."

Negotiating effectively takes regret out of the equation because, when you go for it, you know the answer either way. Then, you can be completely at peace about it with zero regrets.

Now that we've dispelled the most common negotiation fears and mindset blocks, it's time to flip that perspective. Here are the top five reasons you should *always* negotiate your salary:

1. **It takes regret out of the equation.** Your peace of mind is paramount, but if you don't try, you'll never know what might have been.

2. **It's a common (and expected) practice.** Again, companies expect you to negotiate. If you don't, you're leaving money on the table that could have been yours!

3. **It improves your self-worth.** The more you negotiate, the higher your self-worth will climb. As your confidence increases, you'll likely find yourself teaching your friends how to negotiate their salaries. Then you can all be kicking ass, taking names, and making a lot more money together.

4. **Everyone should be paid what they deserve.** You should earn what you're worth and not a penny less. You have the experience, the drive, and the skill set, so the *least* they can do is pay you what you're worth.

5. **To assist those who follow.** Again, you're not just negotiating for you. You're raising the bar for the women and marginalized folks who come after you.

Now that you know *why* you should always negotiate your salary, it's time to get into how you go about doing it.

## RESEARCH

As we covered previously in the "Crushing the Interview" section, preparation is, again, of the utmost importance when it comes to negotiating a salary, and this involves research! In fact, 90 percent of a successful negotiation lies in the research phase. It sets you up for success, so you can feel confident during your negotiation conversation.

## UNDERUSED POWER MOVE

**Choose a Number That Makes You Nervous**
Your magic number should be higher than what you feel comfortable with, but the thought of getting it should excite you!

So, what do you need to research, exactly? Two things: your value in a role and your value in the market. Arming yourself with this data is the key to a successful negosh. Once you've done your research in these two areas, you'll be able to come up with your "magic number."

## HOW TO DISCOVER YOUR VALUE IN A ROLE

Before you can identify your value in a role, you'll need to answer the following questions:

- **How many years of experience do you have in your industry?** The more you have, the higher your magic number should be.
- **How many years of experience do you have with this title?** Regardless of the industry or vertical, the more years of experience you have with a title (or a similar one), the higher your magic number should be.
- **What have you achieved in your industry, and how will it benefit your next employer?** This is where you need to fully buy into yourself. Consider all of your small, medium, and major career achievements, and then list them (you can use your resume as a starting point).

After you create your list of accomplishments, complete with metrics to illustrate them, whenever possible, it's important to keep it on hand. It will be the foundation of your business case, which we'll cover in a bit.

## HOW TO DISCOVER YOUR MARKET VALUE

To identify your value in the market, you first need to find out what the standard rate of pay is for that role, in that industry, and in your geographical location. Here are some tips for finding all of this info:

- **Ask around:** Consult friends, family, or anyone in your network with similar career experience, and ask them how much they're making.
- **Surf the web:** Websites like payscale.com, glassdoor.com, and levels.fyi offer handy ways to research market salaries for your title and industry.
- **Look at different job descriptions for your desired title:** Many of them will most likely share the starting salary or a range right on the listing.

Once you've figured out what your value is in a specific role and your market value, you should have a pretty good idea of what your magic number should be.

## HOW TO ASK FOR YOUR MAGIC NUMBER

It's always better to aim higher than undercut yourself when they ask for your expected salary range. If you do the latter, you immediately put yourself behind and miss out on what they actually would have paid you. It's an unfortunate reality (and a real bummer) that companies operate this way.

At this writing (summer of 2022), the U.S. Department of Labor reports that the unemployment rate is at 3.6 percent, which is historically low. We're also living in the time of the "Great Resignation," a term and era that I appreciate. It's rare that we see capitalism challenged in this way, so I'm savoring it. As employees, we have the power to choose our employer—not the other way around. That's a key mentality to have as you approach your job search and salary negotiation. They need you more than you need them.

We're now going to briefly press rewind and revisit the interview process, because that's where negotiation begins. Typically, the recruiter will ask you very early on in the interview process what your salary expectations are. Does just the thought of being asked this question make you sweaty?

Well, I love it, and I have a feeling you will, too, once you're prepared to answer it. I love this question because it gives me the opportunity to find out if that job is right for me. I don't want to waste their time (or mine) if we aren't aligned on salary. Ultimately, you do want to share your well-researched salary range, but first, you want to respond with something like this: "I'm looking for the right fit and am negotiable. Can you share the salary range?"

You want to ask this question to prevent you from undercutting yourself. Again, all companies try to get you on board for as cheap as possible, so you have to push back to get what you deserve.

Thankfully, salary transparency is becoming more common. It's a huge green flag if they do share the range. Plus, you'll know if your magic number is in that range or not. If it is, you can move forward with the interview process, and raise your magic number to the highest part of their range. If your magic number is higher than the range they quoted, you can say something like, "Thanks for that information, but my salary expectation is a bit higher, at $X. Is there any flexibility?"

If they say yes, great! If they say no, it's important to consider how much of a gap there is between your magic number and their range. It might not be worth it for you to continue the interview process if it's far below your value. One reason you might want to continue the interview process is if you're changing jobs in a major way. In that case, if you can afford to take the cut, it might be worth it. If not, there are tons of other companies who *will* pay you what you're worth, so don't settle!

If they say they're unable to share the salary range, pay attention to the reason why (if they give one), as it could be a red flag. Then, go ahead and share your range. However, make sure your magic number is at the *bottom* of the range to ensure you don't undercut yourself.

Another key part of preparing for a negosh is knowing what else you want to negotiate *in addition to* base salary. Salary is the most important, for sure, but some other key items you can negotiate include:

- Paid time off
- Bonuses (both sign-on and annual)
- Equity and stock
- A remote or flexible work schedule
- Relocation coverage and bonus
- Tuition reimbursement
- Your job title

Everything is negotiable, so think about what matters most to you and prepare to negotiate for those items. Remember, a negotiation is a collaboration, not a confrontation. If they push back on something, that's your cue to negotiate for something else on your list. For example, you might come back to them with something like, "If there's no flexibility on increasing the equity, can we talk about a sign-on bonus?"

## UNDERUSED POWER MOVE

### The Cheddar Getter

This negotiation tip comes in clutch: if you're leaving behind unvested shares at your prior place of employment, negotiate for that amount (or close to it) as a sign-on bonus in your new role. This way, you won't lose that money.

## BUILDING A BUSINESS CASE

Now it's time to build your "business case." This will be based on the list of career accomplishments you already have, and it's the meat of the negotiation you've just prepared for. Your business case is your justification for asking for your worth. In other words, it's straight-up evidence of your absolute badassery. Whether you're asking for a raise at your current company or negotiating your salary at a new job, you need a business case.

First, let's talk about what a business case is and isn't. As its name suggests, it should be all business and not personal. For example, you would *not* include any of the following in your business case as justification for a higher salary:

- "My rent went up this year."
- "I have children now."
- "I'm moving, so I need to make more money."
- "Ted makes more than me." (More on this topic later.)

While these are all important things, companies aren't responsible for your personal life and don't take kindly to this type of justification in a negotiation. This is actually a good thing. A company that cares too much about its employees' personal lives is also likely to have boundary issues, and burn out their employees quickly.

When it comes to your business case, skip the personal stuff and stick only to your career highlights. All of the following would be excellent to include:

- Your years of related experience.
- Your achievements.
- Your specific areas of expertise and the skill set you're bringing to the company and the role.

Your business case is also a powerful antidote to imposter syndrome (more on this in chapter 10). Save it somewhere outside of your work files and emails so you can look at it any time you feel any self-doubt creeping in. Nothing like a detailed list of your achievements to remind you what a badass you are!

Another red flag to be on lookout for in this process is any company that says they don't allow negotiations, period. Luckily, this is quite rare, but if you do encounter it, it would probably be in your best interest to make that your last meeting. A company that refuses to negotiate is also refusing to discuss your achievements and your worth. Imagine how yearly raise conversations would go? They probably don't even have them.

It's not in your long-term best interest to invest in a company that refuses to even invest in a collaborative dialogue with you.

## ASKING FOR A RAISE AT YOUR CURRENT COMPANY

So far, all the tips in this chapter have applied to negotiating salary for a new role. While most of these also apply when asking for a raise at your current company, there are a few nuances to address.

First, when is the right time to ask for a raise at your current company? The truth is, no specific time is necessarily better than any other. What matters is whether you've been working outside your job description, and if you have any role-related achievements to highlight.

Obviously, the timeline in which this happens varies from job to job and person to person. However, it's never too soon to ask for a raise if you have concrete achievements and examples of your impact to cite (just whip out that fabulous business case). This can take merely a few months or much longer.

If you want to be more strategic about timing based on your company's fiscal year, you might want to ask for your raise two months before "budgeting season." When exactly that is varies from company to company, but anyone in your human resources or finance department will most likely know. That would be an ideal time because if you present your business case to your boss ahead of budgeting season, they can then account for the increased spending on your raise when they submit the budget to *their* boss.

When you give them a heads-up, they can factor in the increase. Plus, they won't be able to give you that lame, age-old "we didn't include a raise for you in the budget" excuse.

## HOW TO ASK FOR A RAISE AND GET IT

When asking for a raise, follow these steps to get it in the bag:

1. **Prepare your business case.** As we covered earlier, this is the factual evidence of why you deserve a raise. Remember to include role achievements with metrics wherever possible, as well as any areas you worked outside your job description. Research salaries and establish your magic number.

2. **Schedule a thirty-minute meeting with your boss.** You should state plainly what you'd like to discuss (you don't want to blindside them). For example, something brief and direct like, "I'd like to discuss my career growth and compensation," is great.

3. **Express, present, and ask.** In the meeting, be sure to express gratitude for the experience you've gained while working there, present your business case, and then ask for your magic number.

A stellar way to ask for a raise would be something like, "Based on current market rates and my achievements in this role, could we increase my compensation to \$X? Will you advocate for me?"

This language is very specific for a reason. The use of "we" is intentional, as negotiation is a collaborative effort. "Will you advocate for me?" brings them in as an active stakeholder, and their answer will speak volumes. A great manager knows that elevating their employees also elevates them.

If they say no, well, of course, that isn't what you wanted to hear, but it does give you key information. You're now aware that your boss doesn't support you. Ask for the specific reason why the answer is no, a timeframe for when you can reevaluate, and then schedule that follow-up meeting. If the answer is still no, it might be time to consider speaking with HR, moving to a different team in the organization, or looking for a new job where you'll be paid what you're worth.

Unfortunately, most managers aren't trained to have enlightening conversations about compensation, so there's a decent chance yours will fumble this and/or direct you to HR. In that case, follow their lead. Go wherever you need to go to get your raise.

***

To close out the research stage of negotiating, let's summarize what we've learned. Once again, the key steps in your research stage should include all of the following:

- Identifying your value in the role.
- Researching market rates.
- Establishing your magic number.
- Writing your business case.

## COLLABORATE

Now that you've done your research, it's time to move on to the next step in the negotiation process: collaboration. This is the actual negotiation conversation. If you've done your research and built your business case, this step is actually much easier than you probably think it is. Remember, this company wants to close this deal with you. You've interviewed incredibly well, and they want you on this team. But you're a star, an icon, a legend! They don't just get to hire you without a collaborative discussion of salary. We all know you're not accepting their first offer— that's for amateurs, and you're now a certified pro. This is your moment to highlight your achievements and get exactly what you deserve.

If they make you an offer over the phone, express your gratitude and excitement, and then ask for everything in writing, including the full compensation details, along with any bonus/equity and benefits. Let them know you'll need some time to digest everything, but that you'll get back to them within a few days. After that period, reach out and set up a video call.

If they email the offer, again, respond with gratitude and excitement, and then set up time to talk on a video call. You never want to negotiate over email because it makes it too easy for them to say no, and you end up having to schedule a follow-up call anyway. You want to have this discussion via virtual meeting or phone.

Now the time has come to negotiate . . . for your *life!*

This is the part that feels scary, but it's time to be brave! The more you negotiate, the easier it becomes. Also, keep in mind that this tends to be a fairly short conversation, not some long, drawn-out dialogue. You can keep it short, sweet, and confident.

Here's a sample script I recommend that has an incredibly high success rate:

> *Thank you so much for the offer. I'm excited about the possibility of joining the team! Based on my experience, the value I'm bringing to this role, and my current market rate, I'm looking for $X (your magic number). Can we make that happen?*

Right off the bat, you're expressing gratitude *and* asking for what you're worth, and that's a beautiful thing. Again, it's important to use collaborative language ("Can *we* make that happen?"). From here, depending on how the conversation flows, you'll likely want to share some highlights from your business case, but be sure to give them time to process and respond. Don't be afraid of hearing "no" or complete silence—both are common in a negotiation.

If you get a no, be sure to pay attention to the reason. You might be able to counter or ask for something different, such as:

*A sign-on bonus of $X and a yearly bonus of X percent would get me closer to my target compensation. Can we make that happen?*

The way a company responds during this process is important. Are they collaborative, open, and supportive, or are they combative, negative, and resistant? Pay attention to the signs and how you feel during the process—trust your gut.

Most companies will be collaborative, but if they aren't, it can be a red flag that they're resistant to paying people what they're worth. That could mean more challenges further down the line when it comes to promotions, raises, workload, and burnout. When you're negotiating, keep all of the following in mind:

- **It might not be fully resolved in one conversation.** They might need to connect with someone else in the organization for approval, and then get back to you, which is totally normal.
- **If it goes silent, follow up.** If you don't hear back from them within three business days, send a quick email that says something like, "I'm excited about the prospect of joining this great team. Do you have any updates on the compensation?"
- **Don't ignore red flags.** If you're trying to jump ship from a toxic workplace, the last thing you want to do is join one that's even worse, so again, trust your gut. There are plenty of companies out there that'll not only pay you what you're worth, but will also be thrilled to do so!

Silence isn't something to fear in a conversation, but rather, lean into it, especially in a negotiation. When we get nervous, we tend to want to fill in any gaps in the conversation. However, in a negotiation (and a few other scenarios we'll dive into later), silence is both powerful and necessary.

Post-negosh, take yourself out for ice cream, watch your favorite movie, call your best friend, or do something to celebrate, because you did the damn thing! No matter the result, you advocated for yourself, and that's worth celebrating. It's a success no matter the final outcome because you stood in your power and took action.

The more you get used to negotiating, the easier it will become. It might even feel exhilarating after you get the first one out of the way. You'll probably be able to predict what they might say and be three steps ahead. Your friends will hear about it and want to know how you did it, and then you can teach them (or just let them borrow this book when you're done).

## UNDERUSED POWER MOVE

### The Silence Technique

After you state your case and ask for your magic number, there might be a pause while the other person considers what you've just said. You might be tempted to fill this silence with something like, "But if you can't do that, I'll take the original offer." Please do not do this. It undermines what you've just said, and lets them know they don't have to meet your magic number. Let the silence happen and leave the ball firmly in their court.

# EVALUATE

So, you've researched thoroughly, collaborated beautifully, and now it's time for the final step of negotiating: the evaluation. This is why you always, always get everything in writing. If you negotiated for more paid time off, increased base salary, a sign-on bonus, etc., all of that needs to be sent to you via email for your review. If you're weighing multiple offers, it's time to see how they stack up against each other and which opportunity excites you the most.

If you negotiated and they came back with nothing, you might need to consider if they can afford you; sometimes, the answer is no. In that case, you'll just have to find somewhere that can. If your gut feeling is you're being undervalued, that isn't going to go away if you decide to work there.

If you negotiated and got what you wanted, or even somewhere in the middle, hell yes! Remember this moment, celebrate it, and tell your friends and family. You just raised the bar for yourself in the short- and long-term. You've increased your earning potential substantially, advocated for yourself, and paved the way for those who will come after you. Plus, you got in some great negosh practice that will serve you well in the future.

While we're on the hot topic of salary, it's important to discuss salary transparency, and why it matters. It's a major topic in the cultural conversation lately, and the tide is slowly starting to turn. When we remain quiet about salary, companies retain the majority of the negotiation power. However, if we spin it and start talking openly about how much we make, the negotiation power shifts back to us.

It's not illegal to talk about salary with your coworkers—the National Labor Relations Act protects you. Companies, of course, don't want you to do so because it will reveal any inequities. Very few companies are transparent about salary, and that's intentional. Most often, it's because there's no consistency or formula in the way in which they decide to pay their employees. Some folks would discover that they're extremely underpaid compared to others who do exactly the same job, and obviously, companies don't want anyone to know that.

Now, as we're starting to have a more meaningful conversation about the gender pay gap and pay inequity, it's a great time to ask your coworkers of all genders how much they make. If you think you might be underpaid (unfortunately, the odds are that you are), you can present it like this to a few trusted colleagues: "I'm trying to find out if I'm being paid equitably here. Do you make over or under $X?"

You can dive deeper with them from there, depending on their response. You might also want to reach out to former colleagues who have left the company and ask them what they were making. They might be more inclined to talk about it because the salary was likely one of the reasons they left. What you find out will probably surprise you.

Your colleagues will probably be a lot more willing to discuss salary than you might think, especially if you share common ground. For example, if you're a woman, reach out to other women first. I guarantee if you're thinking about it and feeling dissatisfied, they are too. It only takes one person to light the match and drive positive change from the inside. Unite as a collective and present your findings to the powers that be. Call out the inequities and compel them to answer.

If you do find out someone is making more than you, follow these steps to rectify the situation:

1. **Process the information.** It can be deeply frustrating and upsetting to learn that someone is making more than you, but take a minute before you jump into action.
2. **Confirm.** Is this person in the same role, at the same level, and in the same or similar geographical location as you? If so, it's time to build your business case and present it to your boss.
3. **Lead with your business case, and ask for your magic number.** You might get the pay bump you're looking for on those grounds alone.

# CORPORATE CHRONICLES
## PAY EQUITY

At a previous job, I had a sneaking suspicion that I was being underpaid. When I researched online, I discovered my salary was under the market rate by 30 percent. Yikes! My first course of action was to ask some trusted colleagues in similar roles how much they were making, which confirmed my suspicions. I then made a plan to discuss it with my boss.

I came in with a strong business case that included my accomplishments and impact in the role. I then asked my boss if they could partner with HR to ensure that I was being paid equitably compared to others with the same title—particularly men. I had a suspicion that if the women I asked were making more than me, then the men were making more than them (this turned out to be correct). I also asked if they would prefer me to go to HR directly about this question, just so everything was transparent. I didn't want anyone to think I was going over their head. I was just being curious and collaborative.

After that conversation, I was never given a clear answer, which is a common scenario. I pushed the dialogue as far as I could, but wasn't getting any answers. I decided that if it was this difficult to get the information, and they weren't going to make any effort to pay me my worth, it was time for me to move on.

Although I never got an answer, I'm glad I went through the process and challenged the status quo. It might make a difference for the next person. I also had some interesting conversations along the way, each of which gave me more clarity about the company and made my decision to move on much easier. These difficult conversations ultimately gave me the confidence to ask for what I know I'm worth.

4. **If the step above doesn't work, it's time to mention the salary inequity.** However, when you do this, don't name your colleague. Say something like, "I learned that someone in my same role is making $X. Can you elaborate on why my salary is Z percent lower? Can we make a plan to work together and get my salary to $X?" or, "Can I get a confirmation that I'm being paid equitably?"

It's difficult not to feel angry, frustrated, and disappointed when you find out you're being underpaid, and you would be 100 percent correct to feel that way. I've been there. Something to remember is that it's not always personal. Many companies are disorganized when it comes to compensation, and they might not even be aware of any inequities until you call them out.

A good company will adjust your compensation accordingly. It also makes you feel a bit better when you have a plan to address it. Whether you decide to ask for the money or move on to another job, making a plan will always feel better than doing nothing.

Now, a terrible company will fight you on this, and they'll fight hard. To me, that's a sign to start looking for another job. If they don't value you in this moment, they certainly aren't going to value you in the future. It's time to move on to a place that will pay you what you're worth. They'll be lucky to have you!

If your primary goal is to make more money, you might want to consider changing jobs more often, rather than staying at one employer long-term. In 2016, a survey conducted by ADP found that the biggest salary increases came after employees stayed at a job for two years, but no more than five. The longer you stay past five years, the less of a pay increase you'll get when you do switch jobs.

Unless you're getting frequent promotions, companies typically offer yearly merit increases of only 3 to 4 percent. When you change jobs, though, you're far more likely to get a significant bump. A recent Conference Board survey reported that one in five job-hoppers received a 10 to 20 percent pay increase.

Once frowned upon, the perception of job-hopping has evolved for the better, and millennials and Gen Z have paved the way. Gone are the days when a long list of jobs weakened your chances of getting hired. Today, it's extremely common to see a candidate early in their career with three to five jobs on their resume, and when I do see that, I don't judge. People change jobs frequently for lots of reasons, but the most common are to escape a toxic job or boss, make more money, or to seek out new challenges.

The key is to be intentional about it, so if a recruiter or hiring manager asks you why, you have your reason ready. I find that this topic rarely comes up in an interview unless you've done an *extreme* amount of job-hopping, such as multiple jobs in less than a year.

If you're in the opposite situation and love where you work, and you're progressing, getting promoted, and making more money, that's great! There's no rule that says you *must* change jobs.

However, if your employer isn't keeping up with inflation, offers you barely there yearly increases, or you're underpaid in the market, it's time to consider changing jobs or negotiating at your current one to get what you're worth.

\*\*\*

Now you're well and truly armed with the tools you need to advocate for yourself and get your money! Never forget that a negotiation is a collaboration, *not* a confrontation. The more comfortable you become with negotiating, the more confident you'll be, not only in your professional life, but in your personal life, as well.

# PART II
# CRAFTING

Now that you know how to conjure up a killer resume, interview with finesse, and negotiate your way to triumph, it's time to make an entrance at that new job. The first few weeks and months at your new gig are absolutely vital. It's time to show off those superpowers and craft a new narrative in which you are the main character.

In this section, you'll learn how to communicate confidently at work—both verbally and digitally. We'll also cover some trickier topics, like how to craft strong relationships with your boss and colleagues, including the more challenging ones.

This is the stuff they don't teach you at school, but probably should. There's so much to prepare for, so many scenarios that can throw you a massive curveball at work. Fear not, we will review the most effective ways to respond confidently and professionally.

We'll also break down a process corporate America has gatekept for decades: the elusive path to promotion! If you've ever been denied a promotion, or are just unsure of how to go for one in the first place, you're sure to find this section particularly enlightening and helpful.

If you're looking for helpful tips on making a strong impression and navigating the curveballs of a new job, while also positioning yourself to move up, this section is for you!

# CHAPTER 6
## MAKING A GREAT IMPRESSION

**POWER MOOD MUSIC**

SLIP AWAY
BY PERFUME GENIUS

0:48                                        −2:45

You've landed your dream job, and now you're eager to make a sparkling impression. It can be overwhelming to start a new gig—so many new people, new systems, new restaurant options for lunch, and so on.

The first ninety days at your new job are important because you're not only making an impression, you're also laying the groundwork for making a major impact. You're showing them who you are, demonstrating your superpowers, and why you're a total badass.

Your first three months at a new job can be quite intense and draining, but also exciting. There will be a lot of new information coming at you from all angles, and you'll be doing a ton of observing and active listening. You'll also be asking curious questions.

After that, you'll be able to start implementing and innovating. It's important to make a great impression so you can start things off with a positive flourish. First impressions tend to be lasting, so now is the time to be thoughtful, deliberate, and memorable!

## YOUR FIRST NINETY DAYS: THE BASICS

When you start a new job with a thoughtfully crafted plan and mission, you set yourself up to win. Below are several key ways you can create a blueprint for success during your first ninety days:

- **Listen and learn:** Be an *active* listener, and remember, it's okay not to know everything right away—no one expects you to! Read the room, and try to get a handle on the vibes and culture. Take note of anything that surprises you, and ask questions to uncover the "why" of anything you don't understand.
- **Bring your best self:** Be on time, introduce yourself, and highlight your superpowers. Don't fade into the background. Strike a balance between being self-motivated and seeking support when you need it.
- **Take an interest:** Make an effort to get to know those with whom you'll be working most closely.
- **Establish open communication:** This will help create a bond of trust between you and your team, especially your boss.

Below are a few other things it would be a good idea to familiarize yourself with:

- The company's mission statement
- The company's strategic goals
- The organizational structure
- Internal jargon
- Core competencies, values, and leadership skills

## THE THREE C'S

Three things will be your guiding force during your first ninety days on the job: curiosity, connection, and creation. These create the foundation for your intentional plan to establish yourself at this new organization. Keeping this in mind will also help you maintain control. You'll always know what to do, and how to do it. It's both important and grounding to have a clear plan at the start of a chaotic new adventure because it can help you stay five steps ahead.

## CURIOSITY

When you start a new job, you have to do a lot of listening. There will be orientations, classes, meetings, and lunches. Again, be an active listener and be curious. Asking strategic questions that display your curiosity will showcase both your intellect and passion.

To get things going, here are some great curious questions to ask your colleagues during your first few weeks:

- Who are your go-to people in other departments?
- Who are the folks I should get to know sooner rather than later?
- What's the team's communication style (email, Teams, Slack, etc.)?
- Which project is the most challenging or time-sensitive right now, and why?
- What's everyone's favorite place to grab lunch nearby?

Likewise, here are some excellent curious questions to ask your boss during the first few weeks:

- Which recurring meetings should I be sure to attend?
- Can you walk me through the team org. chart?
- Who should I be introduced to?
- How frequently will you and I meet, and will I drive the agenda?
- What have your highest performers done in the past that stood out to you?
- What are my week-one objectives?
- What are my month-one objectives?
- What expectations do you have for my first ninety days?
- Can we outline my ninety-day goals?

- How do you measure success in my role, and how will my performance be evaluated?
- What is the best way for me to share my ideas?
- What is the best way for me to provide feedback?

It's also a good idea to provide some feedback to your boss on the hiring and training process, given your recent experience going through it. Your perspective is valuable, so if you have some suggestions on how it could be improved, share them.

### SMART Goal Transformation

When setting your goals, you always want to make sure they're specific, and never vague. Typically, you'll be evaluated against your goals, so it's in your best interest that they be specific and clear. You might have heard the term "SMART goal" before, which is an acronym that stands for: specific, measurable, achievable, relevant, and time-based. It's handy for both you and your boss to keep in mind when goal setting. If you have a nebulous goal, your next steps and how to get there will be unclear. The clearer the goal, the easier it will be for you to tackle it step-by-step and achieve it. Don't hesitate to ask your boss and/or other key stakeholders for more clarity. After all, it's your performance on the line, so you want your goals to be achievable, time-bound, and relevant to your role and skill set.

Adding timelines to your goals will help you prioritize and know which work needs to be completed, and when. Be intentional about your timelines, as well—you don't want it all to be due on the same day. Spread it out so it's achievable. Often, your goals might involve other departments, so their priorities and timelines will need to be factored in, as well. So, focus only on what is within your control, because a lot of it won't be. Your goals shouldn't be dependent on others. Focus on the areas in which *you* are best suited to make an impact.

If you disagree with your boss about a goal, don't immediately accept it. Have a dialogue about it, present your point of view, and ask curious questions.

Before a goal has been made SMART, it might look something like this: *Increase attendance at our annual conference.*

However, after that same goal is made SMART, it would look more like this: *Increase attendance at our annual conference by 30 percent. Last year's attendance was 300 guests* (**Specific, Measurable, Achievable**). *By increasing attendee count, we increase brand visibility and generate more leads* (**Relevant**). *Achieve this by sending out a series of four targeted marketing emails, beginning eight weeks before the conference, September 16* (**Time-based**).

The cadence of SMART goals will vary from org to org. Typically, you'll set ninety-day and yearly goals, but they'll often evolve and change over time, as the needs of the business do. Edit your goals as needed, so they remain achievable and relevant. The last thing you want to do is set yourself up for failure. Often, goals are also tied to monetary bonuses, so you want to know you can nail them.

Another great way to display curiosity is to ask "the why" about something. If you notice a process or system during your first ninety days that seems inefficient, ask why it's that way before providing your feedback. A good way to phrase it is, "I'd like to understand why we do it this way." You have to have the basic knowledge first before you can think about potential ways to innovate or improve something. Your perspective as an outsider is important, so don't be afraid to ask clarifying questions; your feedback could be essential to the progress of the team. When you do give feedback, always be sure to provide your "why," as well. It adds detail and backs up your case, which will make your solution all the more convincing and your innovative idea all the more satisfying. For example, you might say something like, "If we implement this, then we will improve our client response time by X."

## CONNECTION

Connecting with your team is so important, and unfortunately, this step often gets overlooked. Within your first few weeks, set up one-on-one meetings with each of your core colleagues and folks from other departments (including department leaders) with whom you'll be working cross functionally. It's important that you to get to know them, including what their strengths are, what they're working on, their communication style, and how you'll work together.

Even more vital, though, is that they get to know *you* and what your superpowers are. This is their opportunity to discover what you're bringing to the table, and what your vision is. This will help ensure you don't fade into the background, but that you're the main character. Doing the work is only part of the agenda if you want to be recognized for that work. It's important to be known and visible if you want to move up and get paid more. Innovative, high-impact work languishes in the shadows of those who self-promote and have internal champions. We'll cover more on this in chapter 9.

Here's a sample agenda for a "get to know your colleagues" meeting:

- Introductions.
- Where you came from and what your role is.
- Ask them which projects they're most proud of.
- Ask them what their top skills/superpowers are, and then share yours.
- What are their current priority projects and goals?
- What are the preferred methods of communication and collaboration?

Remember, this is a dialogue. Ask them these questions, but share your own responses, as well. The goal here is for them to understand the value and skill set that you're bringing to the team. In turn, you'll get to know them, their unique superpowers, and how you best can work together.

You'll be meeting a lot of people over the first couple of weeks, so be sure to practice your intro and be prepared to repeat it a bajillion times. Your intro should include a bit about your prior work experience, your current role at the company, and your superpowers. Adding in some personal tidbits is a great way to find common ground with others ("Oh, you live in Brooklyn? Me too!"). From there, you can start chatting away about whatever it is you both share. Also, you just likely made a new work friend.

People really enjoy talking about themselves (we all love to feel seen and heard), and they'll appreciate the fact that you took time to get to know them in a one-on-one setting. It's often this human element that's missing in corporate settings, so it's refreshing when it happens. You're also setting yourself up for success to promote your work and results, which we will delve into more deeply when we talk about the path to promotion.

Controversial opinion alert: you can make meaningful connections with your colleagues whether you decide to participate in after-hours activities, or not. The truth is, not all of us have the spare time to attend those types of events, and, frankly, not all of us want to. I'm very introverted, and after I've expended a ton of social energy during my workday, I don't have any left. I simply don't have the emotional or mental capacity to participate in an activity after work with my coworkers. Other folks have kids, side businesses, freelance gigs, partners, and/or a million other reasons not to devote extra time to socializing outside of work, and that's perfectly fine. There's no reason to ever feel guilty or apologize for not taking part in work extracurriculars.

A workplace shouldn't be pressuring you to attend social events. We often place this pressure on ourselves (or sometimes, our peers do). Don't hesitate to defend yourself. A simple, "I have other plans," should suffice. I would often say, "I need to prioritize rest and my mental health," and people understood—in fact, some people were even inspired by it! We put in plenty of time at work; your free time is yours, so spend it how you wish.

There's ample time during the workday to connect with your colleagues in meaningful ways. Have breakfast or lunch together and chat about your lives. Use your active listening skills to make connections, and share more about who you are with the colleagues you like and trust. This can make your work life so much more fulfilling.

There might be occasions when you want to attend afterhours events, and that's great too! Keep your options open. Maybe you just moved to a new city and want to meet people and explore the local scene. Or, maybe you're super extroverted and you gain energy simply by being around people. Do what feels right to you, just don't let anyone else dictate how you spend your precious free time.

## CREATION

As you approach the end of your first ninety days, it's time to start making your individual mark. Now that you've been onboarded, done your active listening, gotten to know your boss and colleagues, and found your rhythm, it's time to start leveraging your vision and unique creative stamp. And this doesn't have to be hard or complicated.

When you start at a new company, one probable reason they hired you is because they want your fresh, external perspective on things. As you become accustomed to the systems and processes, you can (and should) thoughtfully weigh in on what you think can be improved, and how. Again, always inquire about the "why" first. This shows curiosity, a focus on outcomes, and a willingness to collaborate. Prove and quantify your "why" and invite conflict, as this will strengthen your output (more on conflict in chapter 11). These are the skills that make you invaluable and are essential to your growth.

Another part of creation is to identify any gaps in your job description. At this stage, you might have ideas around how to best refine your role, so present them to your boss and articulate

**The Art of the Brag Sheet**

A brag sheet is a digital file that you keep separate from your work files. You use it to log all of your achievements, milestones, progress, compliments, positive feedback, and anything else that makes you feel proud. You can then use it later to update your resume metrics, during performance reviews, to write future cover letters, when negotiating for a raise or promotion, and more.

your "why." Explain how the strategic changes you recommend will positively impact the business and your team's goals.

Once your ninety days have come and gone, your focus will shift to making a tangible impact on the SMART goals you and your boss have set. Ensure you have meetings set up with your boss at regular intervals to discuss those goals—for example, thirty-, sixty-, and ninety-day goal check-ins are a good place to start. Don't forget to set up a system for yourself to track your accomplishments, as well.

When we're in the thick of working at a job, it's easy to forget what we're actually accomplishing. It all becomes routine and we're just doing our job. In reality, we're kicking ass, taking names, adding incredible value, and making our mark on our place of employment. When you think about where they were before you joined, and where they are *after* your impact, that's likely going to be a *huge* difference.

We don't always remember all the meetings we led, projects we oversaw, results we drove, people we trained, work we impacted, conversations we ignited, ideas we executed, processes we innovated and improved, and more. When something positive changes or happens, add it to your brag sheet so you won't forget about it. You're making magic at your workplace, so make sure there's a record of that!

# CHAPTER 7

## REPLACING "SORRY" AND OTHER FILLER WORDS

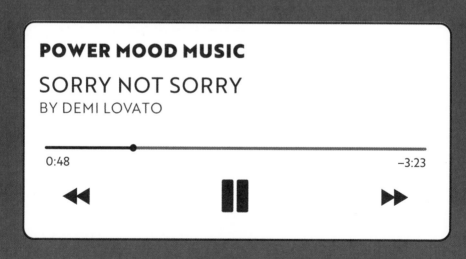

**POWER MOOD MUSIC**

SORRY NOT SORRY
BY DEMI LOVATO

0:48                                              −3:23

Have you ever thought about the number of times per day that you say the word "sorry"? One random Tuesday, I decided to count all my sorries and found that I said it six times that day, which is six times too many. Mine included things like, "Sorry, but could you repeat that?" and even "Oh, sorry," after someone else bumped into *me*!

Let's do a deep dive into the word "sorry." When you overuse it, it starts to lose its meaning, and when you do so at work, it will deplete your confidence in your communication, and ultimately, limit your opportunities to grow.

Simply replacing the word "sorry" can lead not only to improved communication and better results, but, more importantly, to elevated self-worth, a propensity to advocate for yourself, and an amplified presence. In this chapter, we'll uncover why we tend to over-apologize, and how to change our approach.

Over-apologizing can feel like the verbal equivalent of shrinking quietly into a corner. It affects your self-confidence and how others perceive you. It also minimizes the important point you were about to make or the curious question you were about to ask. At work, over-apologizing can make you appear as if you're ready and willing to accept blame, even when something isn't your fault.

As I mentioned, I used to be a frequent over-apologizer. Once I observed how often I was saying "sorry," I also noticed that 100 percent of the time, I wasn't actually the one at fault. I was just saying it out of habit, as a reflex. As women, we're raised to be polite and apologetic (more on this later). I fell very much into the societal norm of an empathetic, apologetic people-pleaser. Sound familiar? I also noticed I wasn't getting where I wanted to in my career, nor was I happy. So, to start with, I made a conscious decision to deliberately go against gender expectations and eliminate unnecessary "sorries."

When I made the decision to start apologizing less at work, I noticed that things started to change. I felt less intimidated and more confident, and my stress levels were lower. I started speaking up more in meetings and sharing my ideas more boldly. I also noticed my colleagues were more dialed-in when I spoke. People started perceiving me as confident and undeterred, although a select few saw me as "arrogant" (more on this later). I felt more charged, powerful, and uplifted, while simultaneously being my usual, empathetic and kind self.

Dropping the sorries felt so great that it led me to re-evaluate my communication overall—both written and verbal. It turns out that letting go of sorry was the gateway to eliminating a ton of other filler words I used out of habit, including "just," "but," and "totally." My communication became more direct and streamlined. As a result, I felt incredibly confident and stopped second-guessing myself. I took ownership and spoke my mind, while still being 100 percent me. In fact, I felt more like myself than ever before. I also started speaking more slowly and intentionally, which encouraged my colleagues and supervisors to lean in and be active listeners.

My increased confidence led me to advocate for myself and get the promotion that I knew I deserved. After that, I started coaching other women to communicate confidently and do the same. I felt like I'd unlocked a workplace secret no one was talking about. Eliminating sorry was just the beginning of a journey that, over time, changed my life, and I know it can do the same for you.

We have to fight against our impulses to do this, however. In a 2021 interview with *Elle* magazine, Dr. Leela Magavi, a psychiatrist and Regional Medical Director for Community Psychiatry in California, revealed that courtesy at all costs is ingrained in women at an early age.

"During childhood and adolescence, girls are socialized to respond to individuals' remarks in a courteous manner, irrespective of the content," Magavi said. "Over time, young girls evolve into women who prioritize other individuals' comfort and emotions over their own."

Being polite and apologizing is a learned behavior. We do it out of habit and, in many cases, out of fear for our safety. When we do speak our minds directly and confidently, society often labels us as "aggressive" or "difficult." This is a systemic issue, and it's not our responsibility to solve it. Many of us are extreme people-pleasers as a result of our upbringing, but, according to Dr. Magavi, we can break the habit by actively choosing to speak our minds. Starting with something as small as eliminating "sorry" can help you break the habitual, people-pleasing pattern.

Women are also often intensely focused on the importance of being polite, even when we're actively being harmed. Constant politeness is a pressure and a burden placed on women from a young age that's rooted in our patriarchal society.

Think about how you feel when you get verbally harassed on the street. There's a distinct inner urge to be polite to maintain your safety (which is 1,000 percent warranted). What you probably want to say is, "Rot in hell, you misogynist failure!" What you probably actually do is immediately look away (maybe with a slight eye roll) and pick up your pace. Similar to the urge to over-apologize, this is also rooted in fear. We fear an unlikely outcome, such as being reprimanded, embarrassed, or even fired. But when we over-apologize, we're inadvertently accepting blame that isn't ours to accept.

Most of the time we say "sorry," it's out of habit because we think it's the polite thing to do, not because it's warranted. At work, the fear stems from the male-dominated leadership environment, which leads to over-politeness and apologizing. When your workplace has very few (or zero) women in positions of power, that fear is real and it's amplified. When you sit in meetings where you're the only woman, when your boss and your boss's boss are men, when you notice the "good ole boys club" lunch crew, it's intimidating and isolating.

And it shouldn't be that way anywhere. According the The Lorman Blog's report, *The State of Women in the Workplace 2021*, women represent 47 percent of the workplace, yet for every one hundred men promoted to manager, only eighty-five women receive that same promotion. And of those eighty-five, only seventy-one are Latinx, and only fifty-eight are Black women.

At the beginning of 2020, women held 38 percent of manager-level positions, while men held 62 percent. The 2020 Fortune 500 list contained 463 male CEOs and only thirty-seven female CEOs, and only 4.6 percent of the latter were women of color.

Additionally, a 2010 study conducted at the University of Waterloo found that out of 183 documented apologies, women offered 75 percent of them. The study also showed that women and men have very different ideas of what constitutes an apology-worthy offense.

Being empathetic is a superpower, but it also makes women more aware of how our behavior might affect others. Unfortunately, it also leads us to apologize even when we aren't in the wrong. Men also just generally feel like they're in the wrong less often than women do.

As most workplaces are male dominated when it comes to positions of power, and the fact that men are less likely to accept blame and apologize, their expectation is the same of others, a.k.a., the people they promote to leadership positions. Those they promote aren't over-apologizing and, in fact, they perceive that as a weakness. They're used to a direct, confident approach when communicating at work.

However, it's not that we should stop over-apologizing just because men don't; we should stop because we aren't at fault. On the flip side, men might want to examine when an apology is warranted, and offer one more often.

The more we over-apologize at work, the more we needlessly break ourselves down. It also sends a message of weakness rather than strength. It limits us if we continuously accept blame, and as a result, we ultimately don't go after a promotion that we clearly deserve or don't raise our hand to take credit for our hard work. The more you say "sorry," whether you realize it or not, your confidence is slowly, but surely, fading.

I encourage you to take an inventory of your "sorries" over the next week or two. Notice how often you use it, when, and why. You might find some interesting patterns you hadn't previously noticed.

Try the following exercise:

1. Write down all of your "sorries" over the next two weeks.
2. Note of how many of those "sorries" were truly warranted (10 percent, 20 percent, and so on).
3. Going forward, stop yourself before you apologize and ask yourself the following questions:
    ◦ Does this apology minimize me or my ideas?
    ◦ Is this circumstance out of my control?
    ◦ Can I flip this and express gratitude instead?

Let's look at some examples of this in action, and why you should lose the "sorry":

- **"Sorry I'm late to this meeting. The last one ran long."** This places blame on yourself for a situation that was out of your control, and puts others in a position to forgive or excuse it. Instead, try, "Thank you for your patience. I'm really looking forward to this discussion," By flipping it and expressing gratitude to those waiting, you don't burden them with forgiveness or yourself with unnecessary blame.
- **"Sorry, but I'm unable to take that on."** If your plate is full, that's not your fault. You don't want to risk the quality of your work suffering or burning yourself out, neither of which is anything to apologize for. Instead of the above, say something like, "My plate is full this week with other priority projects. What's the urgency of this one so I can reprioritize?" Another option would be, "Is the deadline flexible? I'm currently on a deadline with projects A, B, and C."
- **"Sorry to bother you; I just have a quick question."** The sorry immediately undermines whatever it is you were about to say. There's no need to ever be sorry for having a question; it displays intelligence, curiosity, drive, and an eagerness to learn.
- **"Sorry. I really messed that up."** Instead, try, "Thank you for the feedback; I'm on it for next time." You're still owning your mistake and expressing gratitude for the feedback without apologizing for a minor error. It keeps the focus on growth and future, rather than the past.
- **"Sorry, but I disagree."** There's no reason to apologize for disagreeing with someone. You're simply articulating your unique and valuable perspective. Try, "Let's look at this from another angle," or, "I have a different perspective on this."

It's important to recognize the distinction between excessive, unnecessary sorries and worthy apologies. Limiting your sorries doesn't make you a less compassionate person. By reserving sorry for the life moments that truly warrant it, the word will have a different and deeper meaning. It's a heavy word that should be saved for situations that truly call for it. Making a mistake, asking a question, or having a difference of opinion are a few examples of when an apology simply isn't required.

When overused, sorry becomes a filler word, like "just." For example, "Just checking in to see when you can get this report back to me," versus, "Can you please send me the report by (date) for (reason)?" The more we apologize for small things, the more we convince ourselves that we're in the wrong. If I make a small mistake at work, I own it, graciously accept the feedback, and move forward, but you won't catch me apologizing.

Limiting your sorries doesn't change your entire personality; it helps you get closer to who you really are, rather than needlessly shrinking yourself down. I often get asked where confidence comes from, and I firmly believe that eliminating unnecessary sorries was a huge milestone in my own personal confidence journey. It was an important first step to unlocking my power.

When you stop over-apologizing, you'll feel more confident overall, and this will bleed into other areas of your life. You might find yourself speaking up more in meetings or advocating for a promotion, like I did. Or, you might find that other women start asking you for advice on how to be more confident at work. You'll be able to own your mistakes without feeling an inner shrinking or sadness. You'll simply know you made a mistake, and that you'll handle it differently next time.

Additionally, you'll likely find that you're also communicating more confidently with your family and friends, and that those relationships are deepening as a result. It's incredibly freeing to move away from the countless sorries. You'll speak louder, stand taller, and feel more powerful.

Another possible outcome of ceasing to over-apologize at work involves bias. For me, the increased confidence in my communication was well received by 90 percent of my colleagues; however, there were also a small number of vocal dissenters.

When you communicate more confidently and directly, others might perceive you as being arrogant, aggressive, or bossy. If this happens to you, my advice is to call it out in the moment for exactly what it is: harmful bias. When this happened to me, I asked for specific examples of my aggressive or arrogant behavior, and none could be provided. I then asked if I was simply being direct and confident, to which the response was a lot of mumbling, lack of eye contact, and, overall, a bit of an awkward moment. But we have to get comfortable sitting in that discomfort and awkwardness. It's difficult, but necessary, and there's no reason to ever be made to feel ashamed for being a confident communicator.

It's also important to note, however, that I was able to call out bias without worrying about losing my job. Women of color experience bias in the workplace at a significantly higher rate than white women, and might not feel secure enough in their position to challenge the status quo. But should we have to dim our light because of the incorrect perception of a few deeply biased folks? Absolutely not!

That's why it's essential that you call out bias whenever and wherever you witness it; not only will it help you, but it also paves the way for the women who come after you at that workplace.

Eliminating unnecessary "sorries" is an essential step on your journey to self-empowerment. It's also the gateway to better communication overall, both at work and in your personal life. By bowing out of the over-apology game, you're opting in to self-advocacy and choosing yourself. You're also prioritizing your growth, wellbeing, and confidence, and it's about time!

There are other filler words that creep into our communication and get overused at work. Again, "just," "but," and "totally" are a few frequent flyers. When used in excess, these filler words end up becoming qualifiers in our communication, and minimize the point we're trying to make or the question we're trying to ask.

When I started taking a closer look at my written and verbal communication, I noticed I was overusing a lot of qualifiers. When I stopped, I noticed a strong increase, not only in my own confidence, but also in my work productivity, due to the shortened response time from the person I was emailing.

Here's an example of a follow-up email filled with excessive qualifiers:

> *Sorry to bug you again! I just wanted to check in on the email I sent on Tuesday regarding Y project and make sure you received it. Totally understand that you're super busy right now with everything going on, but wanted to circle back with you. Thanks!*

The same email using only direct language might look something like this:

> *Hey! Circling back on Y. It's vital that the team receives X by (date) to ensure the launch timeline stays on track* (**why**). *When can you send this over* (**clear ask**)*? Let me know if there's anything I can do to support you* (**empathy**). *Appreciate your attention to this* (**gratitude**)*!*

There are some major differences between these two emails. The first is not only filled with qualifiers, it's missing the why (a.k.a., the ripple effects of what will happen if the deadline is missed). It's important to include this element and bring it back to the big picture when you're following up. It reminds the other person why it's important, and what the ramifications are. It also gives them crystal-clear evidence that backs up your ask.

Notice also that both emails have a similar friendly tone, but the second is, undoubtedly, more direct and confident. Consider the style of the person on the receiving end and the overall culture of your workplace when figuring out your tone. I find that confidence with a side of friendliness is a great combo for most.

I'm not suggesting you completely change your personality and the way you communicate. If you love exclamation points, warm language, and/or the occasional emoji, by all means go for it! Be you because that is one of your superpowers. However, you can still be you, while simultaneously eliminating any excessive qualifiers and being more direct in your communication. It's a small change that can work wonders for your confidence and presence.

Try this exercise: open your "Sent" email folder, and find one you've sent recently that contains a lot of qualifiers. Using the guidance above, rewrite that email using direct, confident communication. Make sure the "why" and any important ripple effects are clearly stated. Delete "just," "sorry," "totally," and/or any other unnecessary qualifiers. Then, read your new email and note how it makes you feel. Use these new habits in your future emails, and note any improvements in results and productivity.

Raise your hand if you've ever used this common qualifier: "I don't know if this makes sense, but . . . " My hand is *all the way* up. It's time to banish this one forever. First, it doesn't add any value, and even downplays whatever it is you're about to say—and what you have to say is important.

There's no need to qualify your idea, opinion, or contribution. Whatever you have to say is valuable, and I guarantee others will not only think it makes sense, but that it's a great addition to the conversation. No need to take yourself out of a race before it's even started. Share your ideas and questions directly, without qualifying or apologizing.

***

When you're used to being an ultimate people-pleaser, choosing you can feel selfish. Communicating assertively can feel arrogant and being direct can feel bossy, but you have to remember that neither is true. To overcome these ingrained feelings, most of us will have to sit in that slight discomfort until it becomes power. Once you do, however, this will become another incredible new habit amidst the dawn of many. Give yourself the space and grace to evolve into a more powerful version of you, and never look back!

# CHAPTER 8

## BUILDING RELATIONSHIPS AT WORK

**POWER MOOD MUSIC**

SHOUT OUT TO MY EX
BY LITTLE MIX

0:48                                              −4:06

Relationship building plays a big role in career success. When it comes to moving up, ease of communication, and your general happiness on the job, crafting strong relationships can make your life so much easier.

As an introvert, this wasn't something that was immediately obvious to me, nor did it come easily. I had to learn this and gradually put it into practice. The relationships that you craft at work are your key to your success, and it starts with communication.

Establishing a recurring one-on-one meeting with your boss is key for several reasons. First, it will enable you to get to know each other's communication and work styles, and second, you'll also get to know each other a bit personally.

Early on in my career, I used to think that my boss was "too busy" to meet with just me on a regular basis. I thought I wasn't deserving of their time. This is precisely what imposter syndrome looks like. You do deserve their time, no matter what level you're at or how many direct reports they have. A regular one-on-one meeting is honestly the bare minimum they should be devoting to your professional development.

Plus, these meetings work both ways: they also help your boss stay aligned and updated on your work, as well as your goals, wins, and challenges. When they have meetings with *their* boss, they'll often repeat the information you gave them in your one-on-one. This is how they stay informed, and a great boss knows their team's successes are their successes, as well.

The one-on-one also gives you an opportunity to ask strategic questions, and discuss any roadblocks and potential solutions, as well as your career growth. It will also ensure that you and your boss are consistently on the same page, that you're prioritizing your work correctly, and that your workload is balanced. Plus, you'll have a regular opportunity to make your wins more visible to them, so they can start to recognize your superpowers. They need to see that you're making an impact, growing, and evolving. Meeting regularly also allows your boss to guide you through any challenges and support your successes.

Some bosses have more people directly reporting to them than others, and this will be the determining factor for how often you'll meet. It might be weekly, every other week, or once a month, but, ideally, it shouldn't be less frequently than that. To prep for these meetings, you'll typically drive the agenda, with some time at the end for your boss.

Below is a sample agenda for your recurring one-on-one with your boss:

- **Current projects:**
  - Wins
  - Challenges and potential solutions
  - Questions

- **SMART goals check-in:**
  - ◦ Status
  - ◦ Notable changes
- **Feedback**
- **Career goals**

Allow some time at the beginning for small talk. This is a great opportunity to continue to get to know each other and see if you have any common interests. If you do, bam! You have some go-to topics for small talk in the future. This is super valuable if, like me, you tend to be shy or more introverted. My favorite strategy is to find a topic I can connect with someone on, and then lean hard into it. People are always excited to talk about the things they love.

Below is a Venn diagram of my interests and those of a former boss. As you can see, although our passions mostly diverged, we both loved dogs, and that alone provided us with hours of conversation during our regular meetings. If you can find even a sliver of the center of a Venn diagram in common, you're golden!

## A VENN DIAGRAM OF INTERESTS

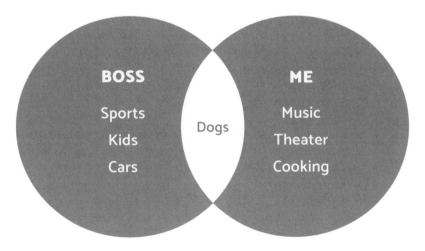

When you arm yourself with a structured agenda, you have a clear framework for every meeting, so you'll both be prepared. I recommend sending them your agenda with some additional details a few days before your scheduled meeting, and ask them if they have anything they'd like to discuss. This way, you can both prepare accordingly. Kicking off the conversation with your recent wins will start the dialogue on a powerful note.

Remember to take credit for your hard work and achievements. In addition to your wins, sharing any challenges you're experiencing, along with some potential solutions, can offer you some big advantages. Specifically, this will illustrate that you're a problem solver, not a problem shifter, which is impressive to bosses and paramount to your own growth.

## HOW TO GIVE AND RECEIVE CONSTRUCTIVE FEEDBACK

Sharing and receiving informal feedback will ensure that you're on a growth track, so you should always ask for it in your meetings with your boss. If you recently led a meeting, or completed a presentation or project, you might ask, "Is there anything I should be approaching differently?" This immediately puts it all out there, but how you respond to feedback also says a lot about you.

Transparent communication in the workplace removes all the guesswork and drama, and allows you to always know exactly where you stand. A good boss will appreciate this direct approach, and it will lead to valuable dialogue. There should also be no surprises come performance review time, thanks to these regular conversations.

Always keep in mind, however, that you can disagree with any feedback that's given to you—just be sure to provide your own examples to counter theirs. This can actually lead to a healthy discussion. Also, if you detect that someone's feedback is subjective or biased, always call it out.

The process for giving feedback like a boss is similar to receiving it:

1. **Be specific.** Always provide specific examples to back up what you're saying. Feedback should be as objective and bias-free as possible.
2. **Frame it as a goal.** Deliver it in a way that's in service of a skill set they can enhance to meet their goals.
3. **Be polite.** Thank them for asking you for your feedback, and offer a compliment or some words of encouragement.

# THE FEARLESS CAREERIST
## HOW TO RECEIVE FEEDBACK LIKE A BOSS

Receiving constructive feedback can be intimidating at first. Your initial reaction might be to shrink down, or even to get defensive, but you must resist those urges.

Try to approach feedback with an open mind. At the bare minimum, it's an opportunity for an interesting dialogue, and at its best, it can be extremely helpful for your personal and professional growth. Being prepared for feedback and having a plan for receiving it openly and graciously can make all the difference.

Follow these steps to receive feedback like a boss:

1. **Ask for feedback on something specific.** "I would love your feedback on how I handled project X."
2. **Ask for clarification.** If they don't provide specific examples, ask for them. These are essential for learning because they remove subjectivity.
3. **Express gratitude.** Say something like, "Thank you for the feedback. I really appreciate it."
4. **Make a plan.** Decide how you will address any issues moving forward.
5. **Call it out in the future.** Whenever you effectively apply the feedback you were given, be sure to point it out.

# CORPORATE CHRONICLES
## HOW TO DISAGREE WITH FEEDBACK FROM YOUR BOSS

Asking for clarification regarding vague, subjective, or outright bizarre feedback is incredibly important. As I mentioned in a previous chapter, a boss once told me she'd heard I was "hostile and aggressive" in a meeting. Needless to say, I was shocked. This caught me off guard, which is exactly what toxic bosses do. No one had ever described me this way before in my life. I was offended, sad, and hurt, and naturally, felt like crying (which would've been a completely valid reaction).

Instead, I said, "This is a bit of a shock to me. Can you please provide an example of when I've been hostile and/or aggressive?" She wasn't able to do so, to which I responded, "This feedback feels biased, and perhaps, sexist. I don't appreciate being called hostile and aggressive without examples. I've been known to share my opinion confidently, but that isn't hostile or aggressive behavior. Additionally, this is secondhand feedback, and I'm not comfortable receiving it, given the immense ambiguity here."

This conversation ultimately went nowhere; still, I'm glad I asked for examples and stood up for myself. Another approach would be to ask, "What are your intentions in giving me this feedback? What skill are you aiming to help me strengthen?"

Women in the workplace, and particularly women of color, often find themselves on the receiving end of harmful, biased feedback. In her 2012 research paper, *Gender Stereotypes and Workplace Bias*, Madeline E. Heilman reported that 66 percent of women receive negative personality feedback on performance reviews, such as, "You can sometimes be abrasive," compared to only 1 percent of men.

Similarly, in the article *Gender Bias at Work: The Assertiveness Double-Bind*, Include-Empower.com reported that women receive 2.5 times more feedback than men do regarding aggressive communication styles. This includes phrases like, "Your speaking style is off-putting."

If you're given feedback that seems biased, unfair, or downright malicious, you might be dealing with a toxic boss.

## IS YOUR BOSS TOXIC?

According to a 2015 Gallup poll, one out of every two employees has quit a job at some point in their lives because of a boss, not the job. The phrase "toxic boss" gets thrown around a lot, but what does it actually mean, and how do you know when you're working for one? Let's find out!

### TEN OBVIOUS SIGNS YOUR BOSS IS TOXIC

Not all bosses are created equal, and if you're dealing with any of the following issues, it's time to polish that resume:

1. All feedback is constructive or negative—never positive.
2. They're combative, put you down, or make you jump through hoops on a regular basis.
3. They're sexist, racist, and/or intolerant.
4. They pile work on you when you're already at, or over, capacity.
5. They micromanage you.
6. They bully or harass you.

7. They play favorites.
8. They're feared by the entire team.
9. They take credit for your work and blame you for their failures.
10. They're completely absent.

## SEVEN LESS OBVIOUS SIGNS YOUR BOSS IS TOXIC

Of course, not every boss is as blatant in their toxicity. Some might be operating in stealth mode, which means it can take you a bit longer to figure it out. However, you'll likely notice some or all of the following signs:

1. They have unrealistic expectations.
2. They don't lead by example.
3. They have zero emotional intelligence.
4. They don't respect your boundaries.
5. They lack vision and/or direction.
6. They feel threatened by you.
7. They don't advocate for you when it comes to promotions and/ or raises.

I've known a lot of people who've stayed at jobs with toxic bosses for far too long. Again, always know your worth. At a bare minimum, you deserve respect, attention, and kindness from your boss. If they aren't even providing you with these basics, it's time to take your talents elsewhere.

If you've just realized your boss is toxic, I recommend taking action. As a first step, talk (or more likely, vent) to a friend about it. Or, if you have the option, speak to a therapist. Not only is this cathartic, but you'll feel validated in your emotions and thoughts. Plus, a professional can give you strategies and techniques for setting boundaries and preparing for potentially difficult conversations.

After the venting stage, if you're in a situation in which you feel you can approach your boss and have a conversation about this, do so.

# CORPORATE CHRONICLES
## DE-NORMALIZING THE TOXIC BOSS

Toxic bosses have been a reality for so long, they've become the norm. I put up with it for what seemed like ages (over two years). I made excuses for them and tried to focus on what I liked about the job, but the truth was my mental health was rapidly declining. I didn't deserve that treatment, and neither do you. It doesn't have to be this way—there is something better out there for you.

The key thing to remember is it's not your fault. Although it sometimes feels personal, try not to take it that way. Document everything they say and do that makes you feel bad, and don't let your list get too long before you speak up about it. If you're comfortable doing so, address them directly. If not, start looking to take your talents elsewhere.

There *are* bosses and companies out there who will respect and support you, pay you well, and provide the type of work environment and flexibility that you need. You're worth it and you deserve it! If your work situation is compromising your mental health, it's time to move on. To de-normalize toxic bosses, we have to start quitting those jobs sooner rather than later.

However, this step won't apply to all bosses, but rather, only those who are at least semi-reasonable and willing to have a conversation about your needs.

Keep the conversation focused on how you feel, and ask curious questions, such as, "I'm concerned about the level of micromanagement in my work. Do you feel I'm not delivering?" or, "Is there some specific feedback you could share to help me improve my performance? I'd like us to get to a place where there is mutual trust because I do my best work with less oversight."

All of these are perfectly reasonable requests, and the way they take it and respond will be very telling. If they're open to talking and working on it, great! If not, they'll make that clear. If they close the door on you, it's time to move on. Expecting and hoping for them to change for the better is a fruitless labor.

Based on how the conversation goes, you should either set a time (two weeks to one month should be good) to check back in with yourself and see if things have improved, or start looking for work elsewhere. Make a list of what you want in a job and a leader, and don't settle.

Review the earlier chapters in this book to update your resume, prep for interviews, and negotiate your new salary like a pro. You deserve to grow, excel, and shine, and if your current work environment isn't providing that, byeee!

## TWELVE SIGNS YOUR BOSS IS ONE OF THE GOOD ONES

If you've been dealing with a toxic boss (or a series of them) for what seems like ages, it would be easy to think that good ones don't exist. Well, the good news is, they *are* out there, and just like the baddies, there are some telltale signs you've lucked into working for a good leader:

1. They provide both positive and constructive feedback regularly.
2. They regularly meet with you one-on-one.

3. They're invested in your goals and professional development.
4. They advocate for you, and your promotions and raises.
5. They're active listeners and help you strategize through conflicts and challenges.
6. They support your career goals and help you achieve them, even if that means you would be transferring to a different team.
7. They bring their whole self to work and encourage you to do the same.
8. They encourage flexible work schedules.
9. They respect your boundaries and have some of their own.
10. They have a clear vision for the future.
11. They lead with empathy and by example.
12. They make themselves available for questions and mentorship.

## FIVE TOXIC BOSS ARCHETYPES AND STRATEGIES FOR STANDING UP TO THEM

There are many types of bad bosses, but we're going to break down some of the most common. You might recognize a past or current boss on the upcoming list. One of my many bones to pick with corporate America is with how companies train their managers, or rather, how they don't train them at all.

Too often, they don't train bosses how to manage people, which is the most important part of their job. Most of the bosses I've worked for were good at the technical (or hard) skills required for their job, but not the people-management (soft) skills. In that area, they were all batting zero (the first and only sports metaphor in this book. Okay, there might be one more).

The first step is recognizing that your boss is toxic and affecting your work and mental health in a negative way. What happens next is up to you, and how you feel about it. If you think you can handle approaching them and opening up a dialogue about it, we'll cover some strategies and conversation guidelines for doing just that in the following sections. In some cases, though, you might feel that they wouldn't be receptive to what you have to say, in which case I recommend planning your exit strategy. It's not your responsibility to change a toxic boss or situation.

However, if you're ready to tackle this sitch, let's look at how you can approach just about every type of toxic boss out there.

## THE NONEXISTENT BOSS

This boss is a ghost. The Nonexistent Boss flakes on your one-on-one meetings and takes forever to respond to your emails—if they ever do at all. They rarely offer you any type of feedback and, if they do, it has virtually no detail or substance. Basically, they might know your name, and that's about it.

To open up a dialogue with a ghost boss, try something like this: "I've been feeling a bit lost lately since we haven't been able to connect one-on-one. I want to ensure we're aligned and that I'm delivering on my goals. Could you give me some feedback so we make a game plan?"

## THE MICROMANAGER

The Micromanager will make you *wish* you had a Nonexistent Boss. This boss hovers hard. They might ask to screen your emails before you send them (yikes!), interrupt you when you're in meetings (oof!), or nitpick every aspect of your presentation (argh!). And I know you worked hard on that presentation. Micromanagers want to control things.

However, there are a few ways you can disarm and politely call them out. For example, you could say, "Are there any issues with the quality of my work overall? Lately, I've been feeling micromanaged, and it's making it difficult for me to succeed.

I'd love for us to reach a place of mutual trust so the current level of oversight is no longer necessary."

## THE CREDIT STEALER AND/OR BLAME SHOVELER

The Credit Stealers really frustrate me. If you've ever had to deal with one, you know exactly why. They take credit for your work as if it was their own, even if they didn't do anything, except maybe sign off on something. Then, they have no problem actually being celebrated for the hard labor *you* put into the project. This is sad.

Essentially, they don't realize that shining the light on and celebrating you is a fantastic reflection on them. Instead, they suck all the energy out of a room and steal the credit from those who actually did the work.

It takes some serious moxie, but I highly recommend calling this out in the moment during a meeting. For example, you might say something like, "To clarify the roles and responsibilities for this project, I led A, B, C, and so-and-so managed X, Y, Z."

It's a shame, but sometimes, you have to jump in and *take* your credit. This is important because when it comes time for raises and promotions, the leadership needs to know about your contributions.

Alternatively, you can approach your boss privately and say something like, "When you took credit for my work during the executive meeting, that made me uncomfortable. I was really proud of what I put into that, and I felt like my hard work was erased."

While the similarly flavored Blame Shoveler doesn't take credit for your work, they blame you for *their* mistakes. This is cowardly, for sure, and, like the Credit Stealer, this type of boss also typically has very low self-confidence. They think that placing blame on others will make them look better, but their team knows otherwise.

Sometimes, a simple curious question is all it takes to put this boss in their place. For example, you might say, "In the meeting on Friday, why was I thrown under the bus regarding Project B? That made me uncomfortable." Unfortunately, this pattern of behavior will likely continue.

Remember, it's not your responsibility to change them, and if you don't have the emotional capacity to hold them accountable, you don't have to. Instead, document their behavior and consider going to human resources (if you can go in as a unified front with other colleagues, that would be best). Or, just make a plan to find another job.

## THE TYRANT

The Tyrant boss is the most difficult to work with and approach. They're challenging to reason with, and while the other toxic archetypes all have varying degrees of this (a.k.a., lack of people skills), the Tyrant is the toxic boss that rules them all. Generally, this person spends all their time at work trying to make everyone else miserable. This leads to a team of people who are overworked, terrified, and anxious.

This is the boss who puts you down, picks apart your work, offers zero guidance or training, and is always in a sour mood. It's like they've never managed a person a day in their life, but they somehow have a team of eight great people under them. At their absolute worst, they subject you to some type of harassment, which is serious.

If you find yourself in this scenario, document what happened and go to human resources immediately. If HR tries to brush it off, which unfortunately, is something that tragically still happens, go straight to your local labor board and/or take legal action, if possible. The age of tolerating harassers is over. You should never accept that kind of treatment from anyone, let alone a supervisor at work. We'll take a deeper dive into handling harassment, discrimination, and microaggressions later in this chapter.

## THE COMBO-PLATE BOSS

If you read all of the above and found yourself thinking, "Wow! My boss does all of those things," I'm so sorry. What you have is a Combo-Plate Boss. This boss is a combination of all of the toxic boss archetypes. Perhaps they're a strong dose of Micromanager with a pinch of Tyrant, or they have a Credit Stealer sun with a Blame Shoveler rising.

The Combo-Plate will keep you guessing when it comes to which sampler of toxicity they'll be serving up each day, so you'll never know what you're gonna get. However, you can use the suggested approaches in the previous sections to deal with their worst offenses.

# YOU HAVE A TOXIC BOSS—WHAT NEXT?

So, you've identified that you do, indeed, have a toxic boss. What should you do next? Well, first, it's important to ask yourself a few questions:

- Is the work experience worth it?
- Can you write your own story here, despite your boss?
- Is your boss making your life so miserable that you can't stand it?

If you have the emotional capacity, and you think your boss would be open to a discussion, I highly recommend it. Does it take guts to talk to your boss about these things? Absolutely! Will it give you the answer you're looking for? Absolutely! They'll either take your feedback to heart and change their behavior *or* they'll do nothing, in which case you'll know what you need to do. Either way, you'll get an answer.

A toxic boss doesn't deserve you on their team, but when you're in the situation, it's easy to feel trapped. It's happened to all of us—

myself included—and I strongly recommend that once you smell even the slightest whiff of toxic garbage, you start a list of incidents on your personal computer, phone, or a sheet of paper. Document their behavior, and how it makes you feel.

When you're working under a boss like this, it's easy to dismiss their behavior as a one-off, or even place blame on yourself for not being "tough enough." It's much harder to dismiss it when you look at your notes and see that it's a clear pattern. Don't let that notebook rack up too many examples, either—as soon as you notice your work is being impacted, that you're feeling drained or unhappy, or your mental health is suffering, take action.

When you have a toxic boss, it can feel isolating, so if you have trusted colleagues, talk about it with them. If it's happening to you, it's most likely happening to them, too. See if you can harness the power of the collective and come together to create change. The collective is larger and more powerful than one toxic boss, so unite. If this isn't an option, talk to your friends, family, or a therapist, but don't suffer in silence.

Next, make a game plan. Building an exit strategy puts you in control of the situation. Only you can decide when it's time to cut ties and move forward, but whenever you're ready, carve out the time to apply for jobs. Reach out to your network and ask if they know of any opportunities. Dealing with a toxic boss or workplace and having to spend any remaining energy applying for jobs can be quite taxing. That's why I suggest applying for jobs strategically—don't apply for twenty a day just to see what sticks. Tailor your resume and cover letter, and only apply for positions you're truly excited about. Why waste your precious energy applying for jobs that don't interest you?

In the meantime, if you can, take as many days off as possible: vacation days, mental health days, sick days, you name it. You need time to rest and refuel. When you're in a toxic situation, a great remedy is to spend time doing things that bring you joy and make you feel like you. For me, that's drinking my favorite tea (jasmine with honey), watching my comfort TV shows (hello, *Scrubs* and *RuPaul's Drag Race*), and chitchatting and laughing with people I care about. The same applies after you quit a toxic job, as well; if possible, take a week or two (or more) off between jobs. You need time to heal.

Be sure to identify your boundaries and non-negotiables (see chapter 12). Also, consider what you can take from this experience and apply in your next job. Toxic bosses test and try our boundaries, which can help us further unlock what's most important to us.

### FIVE SIGNS IT'S TIME TO START LOOKING FOR A NEW JOB

Sometimes, we get comfy (or just used to) things that are harming us because we fear the alternative. It's the devil you know versus the devil you don't. From experience, I can tell you there is something better out there for you.

If any (or all) of the below resonate, it's time to start looking for a new job:

1. Your mental and/or physical health is being negatively impacted.
2. You're no longer learning and growing.
3. You're underpaid and/or undervalued.
4. Your workplace rewards burnout.
5. You can't be yourself at work.

## DEALING WITH DIFFICULT COWORKERS

A coworker once asked me, "How do you keep a poker face when people are saying such outlandish, incorrect things during these meetings?" My response was, "My peace is paramount, and I don't let anyone I work with disrupt that. It's not worth it."

Bosses aren't the only people who can be difficult to deal with at work. Sometimes, we have to work or collaborate with folks we don't necessarily vibe with. When it comes to dealing with difficult coworkers, here is some of my best advice:

- **Don't take it personally:** This person is most likely acting this way because of their own internal issues. It probably has nothing to do with you.
- **Accept that no one likes everyone, and that's okay:** You can't please all of the people all of the time, nor should you try. Also, if you're struggling to get along with someone, chances are, other folks are, too.
- **Mindfulness is key:** A really toxic person can only drive you nuts if you allow them to, and usually, that's exactly what they want. Don't give them the satisfaction of getting a reaction out of you. Put your peace up high on a pedestal where no one can reach it.

Try not to waste your energy on anything you don't have to. One of my favorite phrases is, "Not my circus, not my monkeys." At a toxic workplace, I was especially conscious of *not* giving it everything I had because I needed to save some energy for me. Find a balance here, and do what works for you. Ultimately, don't give them too much—whether it's your emotions, hard work, time, or mental capacity.

Think of it like a glass of juice: when you start each workday it's full, but it's up to you whether you sip or chug. What you *don't* want to do is pass your glass freely to someone else—after all, you don't know how much they're going to drink. And this is your juice. Always make sure there's some juice left for you at the end of a hard day's work.

# DEALING WITH DISCRIMINATION

The worst type of workplace is one that perpetuates or tolerates
any type of discrimination. Unfortunately, all we have to do is
look at this collection of statistics published on Nasdaq.com in
2022, to realize that many people already have, or will, experience
discrimination at work:

- 55 percent of workers have experienced discrimination at their
  current company.
- 61 percent have witnessed discrimination happen to others.
- 24 percent of Black employees, and 24 percent of Latinx and
  Hispanic employees have experienced discrimination at work
- 46 percent of LGBTQ+ workers have experienced
  discrimination at work.
- 54 percent of those who reported the incident had the matter
  fully resolved.
- 32 percent of employees who experienced discrimination did
  not report it.

## WHAT WORKPLACE DISCRIMINATION LOOKS LIKE

Discrimination can and does happen in many forms, both in life and
work. This list barely scratches the surface, but some of the most
common types of workplace discrimination include:

- Being paid less than colleagues in the same role.
- A lack of women—especially women of color—in leadership roles.
- A supervisor or colleague using racial slurs.
- An employer that refuses to make accommodations for those
  with disabilities.
- An employer that refuses to accommodate religious beliefs.

- A boss who gives all the best projects to the white men on the team.
- A supervisor or colleague who harasses you.
- An employer that retaliates if you file a complaint with human resources or legally.
- An interviewer who asks your age, race, gender identity, marital status, or any other personal (and irrelevant) information.
- An employer or interviewer who asks if you're planning on having children any time soon.

## WHAT WORKPLACE MICROAGGRESSIONS LOOK LIKE

As you might have guessed, microaggressions are less obvious than other forms of discrimination, but they're just as offensive. Again, the following is a nonexhaustive list, but some common examples of microaggressions include these types of statements, questions, and behaviors:

- "Where were you born?"
- "Can I touch your hair?"
- "Racism doesn't exist at this company."
- "You don't look gay."
- "My best friend is Asian."
- "Your name is difficult to pronounce. Do you have a nickname?"
- Men who interrupt women during meetings.
- Asking only the women in the office to make coffee, take notes during meetings, or run errands.
- Intentionally using the wrong pronouns for someone.
- Mansplaining, a.k.a., a male coworker condescendingly explaining a concept to you.
- Telling a woman she should "smile more," "tone it down," or be "less aggressive," "less direct," or "more likable."
- Any comments on your appearance, including how you dress or style your hair.

## GENDER DISCRIMINATION IN THE WORKPLACE

At a previous job, I once sent a very simple email after a big town hall meeting, in which I wrote:

> *Great meeting today. I noticed in the leadership shout-outs segment, of the ten leaders recognized for their hard work and top performance, only two were women. Representation matters. Going forward, I know we can do better.*

I, perhaps naively, did not anticipate the response I was about to receive from someone very high up in the company. His response was quite long and contained the following list of rebuttals:

- "I think instead of critiquing, we should focus on the progress we've made with regard to gender diversity and women in leadership."
- "There were actually three women mentioned, not two, which is 30 percent."
- "Industry-wide, we're actually doing better than a lot of other companies in terms of women in leadership."

This particular type of response is problematic because it employs a concept called DARVO, which stands for Deny, Attack, and Reverse Victim and Offender. Coined by Jennifer Freyd, a psychology professor at the University of Oregon, DARVO is when a perpetrator of wrongdoing, after being held accountable, attempts to reverse the blame to the victimized party. It's often used by perpetrators of sexual abuse.

Oof! Not a great look for the leader of a multimillion-dollar company. Rather than simply saying, "Yes, we can do better moving forward," he seemed to take it personally and felt the need to DARVO the absolute heck out of me. This is a common response of perpetrators of wrongdoing. In an effort to avoid any and all accountability, they attempt to make themselves the victim. It's also an attempt to lessen any responsibility to respond to and correct the issue and confuse things by making the victim feel bad for saying anything at all.

Unfortunately for him, I've been around this block, and immediately recognized this misogynist, harmful tactic. Was I surprised? No. Was I disappointed? Absolutely. When we go out on a limb like this, we want to be heard, but instead, I was shut down and belittled. I wish I could say this was an outlier, but I've experienced situations like this again and again.

What I do know is that I didn't (and still don't) regret sending that email. His response actually proved my *entire point*. I had attempted to address the problem of gender discrimination at the company. Rather than accepting any accountability, or even acknowledging that this might be a problem, he chose instead to blame me for bringing up the issue. His goal was to shut down the conversation, and I'm sure he thought it had ended there—but I wasn't finished.

I responded to his harmful rebuttal with, "It's precisely this type of response that prevents women from coming forward when we experience discrimination." I left it at that and, unsurprisingly, didn't receive an email back.

This wasn't the last time I discussed gender equity with this person, and I'm certain it was this initial email exchange that sparked that. Although, I wasn't sure what would come of it, I knew it was important that I say something. I couldn't let him silence me and the other women at the company.

Progress isn't always linear, which is why I always recommend that you call out bias, discrimination, and inequity whenever you see it. You might not love the response, but any way you slice it, you're making an impact.

## How to Be an Ally to Women in the Workplace

In the fight for workplace equity in terms of pay and position, women need men to be on their side. Below are some concrete ways you can support women at work:

- **Use appropriate language:** Avoid using harmful, biased terms, such as "intimidating," "bossy," or "aggressive," to describe confident women.
- **Call out harassment and discrimination in the moment:** Never be a silent bystander and always report any incident afterward.
- **Call out interrupters:** If someone interrupts a woman during a meeting, say something like, "Hey, I don't think she was finished speaking."
- **Give credit where credit is due:** Point out when a woman's ideas and contributions have made a difference on a project, especially if someone else tries to take the credit.
- **During promotion season, speak up:** Recommend all the great women you work with, and especially women of color.
- **Be conscious of who's at the table during important meetings:** If you notice there are zero women at a conference table, call it out and make suggestions to fix it.
- **Take on "office housework" duties without being asked:** When it needs to be done, refill the coffee, or volunteer to organize team events or take notes during a meeting.
- **Do your best to ensure equal opportunities:** Double-check that women, and especially women of color, have equal access to any mentorship opportunities.
- **Be aware of the impact of gender bias:** Pay particular attention to how it affects performance reviews and insist they be evaluated by an objective third party.

- **If you're in a leadership role, mentor women:** Do what you can to help women, and especially women of color, advance within the company by giving them special projects, clients, or assignments.

## WHAT TO DO IF YOU'RE SUBJECTED TO DISCRIMINATION AT WORK

If you feel safe doing so, you can follow these steps to hold someone accountable for any type of workplace discrimination:

1.  **Act quickly.** Call out the behavior in the moment. Express that you're uncomfortable and explain why what was said or done is harmful. If it happens to someone else, offer them your support, and if they haven't yet done so, calmly explain to the room why the incident was harmful or offensive. Later, check in with them to see how they're feeling and if they need further support.
2.  **Document and report.** Write down exactly what happened and who was involved, including the date and time. Then, share it with your boss and human resources.
3.  **Escalate by reporting the incident(s) to the Equal Employment Opportunity Commission (EEOC).** If human resources can't (or won't) resolve the issue, and you feel unsatisfied or disappointed, you can report your employer to the EEOC.
4.  **File a discrimination lawsuit.** If the EEOC is unable to resolve the issue—and especially if you've lost your job or incurred any other type of loss or harm due to the incident(s)—you might want to consult an employment rights attorney about filing a lawsuit against your employer.

Given the statistics we covered earlier, the odds are good that you've either experienced or witnessed some form of workplace discrimination at some point in your career.

First, it's important that you realize that you're definitely *not* alone, and that it is *not* okay. Along with the Great Resignation and salary transparency movements, workers are also starting to call out employers in ways they haven't in the past, which is progress.

The fact is they want you to remain silent and do nothing, so they don't have to change anything. When you speak up about discrimination in the workplace, you're not only standing up for yourself, but also for everyone who will come after you. It sets a precedent that will (hopefully) benefit the next person who faces discrimination at that company.

However, when you put yourself on the line like this—whether for yourself or someone else—it tends to take an emotional and mental toll. Be sure to talk to a friend, family member, or therapist about what happened. Or, reach out to your community and share your story; you'll likely hear many that echo your own. Also, be sure to take some time off to rest and do things you enjoy. Put yourself first, and always remember that you are powerful.

# CHAPTER 9

## TACTICAL AMBITION

**POWER MOOD MUSIC**

HARD
BY RIHANNA (FEATURING JEEZY)

0:48                                                     −4:10

◀◀            ⏸            ▶▶

This is a very important chapter in this book, and it's also quite personal to me. I knew nothing about tactical ambition at the beginning of my career. To this day, it's like some ancient corporate secret that only white men know about and utilize. Tactical ambition means taking specific actions to secure a promotion.

Once again, you have to advocate for yourself because, most likely, no one else is going to do it for you. Tactical ambition isn't just about delivering results, but also how well you promote those results, advocate for yourself, and articulate your case for promotion.

This all might sound like some weird corporate game, and it kinda is. However, advocating for yourself can also add deep value and meaning to your life by boosting your confidence. It's not all a ruse, and it's definitely not a waste of time.

If you want to grow, move up in your career, and boost the percentage of Fortune 500 female CEOs from 8 percent to 100—this chapter is for you!

How do you know when you're *ready* for a promotion at work? It's actually sooner than you might think. If you wait until you are 100 percent ready, it'll probably be too late. Remember the manager and CEO gender stats we reviewed earlier? Men currently hold 62 percent of manager positions, while women hold only 38 percent.

Men are being promoted based on their potential much sooner than women. They also have the confidence, and audacity, even, to ask for that promotion. Frankly, some just get it handed to them, even if they're unqualified.

People tend to promote people who resemble themselves, so men tend to promote other men, whether they deserve it or not. This is why I highly recommend you don't wait until you're 100 percent ready for that promotion—ask sooner!

If you often find yourself doing any of the following, it's time to kick your tactical ambition into high gear:

- Answering your peers' questions about the work.
- Training or mentoring others on your team.
- Achieving results.
- Nailing the work your boss delegates to you.
- Regularly assisting (and being relied on by) folks in other departments.
- Conquering and/or working beyond the requirements of your job description.

## UNDERUSED POWER MOVE

### Tactical Ambition Is a Necessity

I'm sorry to tell you this, but the common narrative that "if you work hard and do a great job, you'll get promoted" is a lie. I wish it were that simple, but the truth is that you **must** advocate for yourself to get promoted. And sure, you should work hard—but not **too** hard.

There are three phases of tactical ambition, but at the end of those lies your promotion and pay raise—woo-hoo! This process doesn't have to take a long time to complete, either; in fact, it shouldn't. It's possible to be promoted within three, six, or twelve months of starting a new role. That's why it's never too soon to get started on phase one of your tactical ambition plan.

## TACTICAL AMBITION PHASE ONE: ESTABLISH ROLE EXPERTISE

Some organizations are more transparent than others when it comes to their promotion process. If you feel like you're navigating a murky, dark, scary cave, you're not alone. Go forth into the unknown, my friend! This is how we do it, and I'm right there with you.

Prior to getting promoted, you first need to establish role expertise in your current job. Basically, you need to become an expert on each of the responsibilities outlined in your job description, so make sure you have a copy of it handy while reading this section. You'll want to review it line by line, and ensure you're delivering on all fronts. If your workplace also has Key Performance Indicators (KPIs) or competencies attached to your role, you'll want to know where you stand on all of those, as well. KPIs can be anything from sales numbers, and customer happiness scores to website views or link clicks. Ask your team leader or someone in human resources about these if you can't find the answers on your own.

Some other elements of establishing role expertise include taking the initiative, being an idea person, and leading your peers. Now, you might be hesitant to do the latter at first, but hear me out on this one. If you're afraid of stepping on someone's toes, how can you set yourself apart? If you know what you're doing and have the people skills to do it, why not lead? The more others start seeing you as a leader, the more obvious it will be that you should be promoted to the next level.

If you're unsure how to start leading your peers, below are some tips to help you ease into it:

- **Own your superpowers:** Know your areas of expertise and skill set, and add value to your colleagues' projects accordingly. If you also excel in any of your coworkers' areas of opportunity, help them grow.
- **Empower others:** Lead projects on your team whenever possible and, when you do, hold others accountable, while always remaining on their side. This will motivate them to deliver great results as you propel yourself to do the same. Let everyone know they can always come to you with any questions. If possible, mentor a teammate, or even someone on another team.
- **Be visible:** Develop a strategic relationship with your boss, so that you become their go-to person. Ask your boss if you can sit in on higher-level strategic meetings and/or lead team meetings when they're out of the office. Always have a prepared agenda for all meetings, as this displays initiative and leadership.

When it comes to developing a strategic relationship with your boss, I know firsthand that this can be challenging and intimidating. One of the best ways to get ahead in the corporate world is to become adept at knowing your colleagues' superpowers. A successful team is dependent upon the superpowers of its members, so you all need to have complementary, diverse skill sets. This goes for your boss as well. What makes them tick? What are they great at? What are they not so great at, and how can you be the person to fill in that gap?

It sounds complicated, but it doesn't have to be. As I covered previously, make sure you schedule regular (weekly, biweekly, etc.) one-on-one meetings with your boss. You need to get to know them, and they need to get to know you. Also, always do what you can to ensure they're present to see your stellar work in action. For example, if you're hosting a big presentation, make sure they're invited so they can bear witness to your greatness. If you receive some awesome feedback from a coworker or superior, be sure to forward it on to them without hesitation. You already know how fantastic you are, it's your boss who needs to see the evidence, so make sure they do!

## TACTICAL AMBITION PHASE TWO: PROMOTE YOUR IMPACT

This leads us into the most important step on the path to promotion—promoting your impact. It's also the part that's talked about the least, given the age-old assumption of how one climbs the corporate ladder: "Put your head down and work hard." Growing up, you probably heard this from your parents, teachers, and friends—and it's BS. If you're content where you are, then, by all means, follow this advice.

However, if you want to advance your career, make more money, and be recognized for what you do, the secret is you don't actually even have to work *hard*; you simply have to promote the work you do.

This isn't easy to do at first because most of us aren't used to taking credit, touting our accomplishments, and promoting our successes; however, I challenge you to try it. Not only will it boost

## UNDERUSED POWER MOVE

### Raise Your Voice and Work Smart

The old "Put your head down and work hard" adage only leads to burnout and being passed over for promotions. Being visible is more important than how much you do, so work just hard enough to make an impact. If you worked on a project that yielded great results, you need to not only take credit for it, but also make sure that the "powers that be" are aware of your excellence.

your confidence, but it's also good for your boss and other key stakeholders to know about the impact you're making. Then, when it comes time for performance reviews and promotion discussions, they'll have some specific examples of your acumen.

If you're unsure whether you should promote your work, ask yourself the following questions:

- Does everyone who needs to know about this know about it?
- Is this useful for other teams?
- Is the outcome relevant to a company-wide goal?
- Is the outcome exceptional?
- Does this prepare us for a future challenge?
- Was my storytelling influential in decision making?
- Does the complexity of my work make it singular?

If you answered yes to any of the questions above, it's time to promote your work and get phase two of your tactical ambition plan rolling! Below are a few ways you can do it:

- **Share your wins and positive feedback with your boss regularly:** Once again, whenever you receive positive feedback from a colleague or leader in the organization, save it in a designated folder and forward it on to your boss. Always keep them in the loop about your successes, and never assume they already know (they usually don't). You can add something like, "This made me really proud," or, "Check out this great feedback from Rosa!"
- **Host impact meetings with your boss and other key stakeholders:** These will give you the opportunity to display the results of projects via a PowerPoint presentation, charts, or graphs. This clearly shows your boss where you started and ended on a project. Tie-in how your work has positively impacted the strategic plan or company goals. Highlighting

your effect on the big picture is key because it shows how your work is helping to move the business forward. Be sure to send a follow-up email with a summary afterward.

- **Create and track Key Performance Indicators (KPIs) for all initiatives you own:** This gives you hard data to back up your results (and also provides you with some prime metrics for your resume and brag sheet content). Nothing is too small to include!

## 5 | POWER MEMO — Silence does not serve you.

If any (or all) of the above feels like bragging to you, keep in mind that your boss most likely doesn't know exactly what each team member is working on and the impact they're having on the business. After all, they most likely manage at least several people and have their own work to focus on. Managers can also sometimes focus on the wrong things because they haven't been properly trained, especially when it comes to how to motivate people (more on this later).

As a result, the burden falls on you to close this gap and promote your work and the impact it's had. Don't assume, like I did, that it will speak for itself. I've discussed this with many friends and colleagues over the years, and we've all had similar experiences. We worked hard and hoped for the best, without even thinking we needed to advocate for ourselves and promote our work. I saw men around me being promoted for their potential all the time, so I just assumed it would work the same for me. Unfortunately, that wasn't the case.

When I realized I wasn't getting the promotion I knew I deserved, that's when I started advocating for myself and asking questions. I built a strong business case, researched market data, and presented it to the higher-ups. It took about two years of presenting my case, banging on various doors only to be told no, and refusing to give up before it finally happened. In hindsight, I should have quit sooner and gotten that promotion elsewhere. However, I'm glad I went through it all because now, my experience is helping other women know when to say enough is enough.

There's no doubt that this part of the career system is deeply broken. It's set up for white men to promote other white men, and for anyone outside of that identity, especially Black and Latinx women, the journey up the proverbial ladder is *very* different. You have to kick down those doors and advocate for yourself, which can be exhausting. You might also need to call out the elephant in the room as you're doing it and just say, "If I were a white man, would it be this hard?"

I hate that women have to fight so hard for the promotions and raises they undeniably deserve, while less-qualified white dudes continue to be handed the corner office. But this is why I do what I do. We have to infiltrate the system, call out the bias, and tear it down from the inside.

Months after being denied a promotion and raise, I finally confided in a female colleague, who asked why I hadn't told her sooner. Then, all the women could have leveraged our collective power and knowledge. Her question stopped me in my tracks because I hadn't even considered this before; I'd just kept it all inside and suffered in silence. If you find yourself in a similar situation, by all means, don't keep it to yourself. Trust in and share it with your community and/or network of women, so they can support and uplift you. Alone, we are fiery, but together, we are incendiary!

Along with the challenges that come with advocating for yourself, there are also some intrinsic benefits. It is, in fact, quite the power mood! When I first started promoting my work and sharing my accomplishments with my boss, there was an adjustment period for both of us. I encourage you to embrace the discomfort, step into your power, and get comfortable with your newfound confidence. I'm behind you! You work hard, you deliver results, and people should know about it. Plus, when it comes time to build your case for a raise or promotion, the work will all be done and your brag sheet will write itself.

## TACTICAL AMBITION PHASE THREE: OBTAIN THE BUY-IN

You've established role expertise and have been promoting your impact, but now it's time to talk to your boss and get them on board. This is known as the "buy-in." After seeing all your results, you might think they'll simply offer you that promotion—and they just might! If so, you have yourself a great leader there.

However, more often than not, they won't. It often takes more than quantitative evidence of your excellence to get a promotion. This is not necessarily because your boss doesn't believe in you, it could be they simply don't know you *want* it. This is why you need to make them aware of what's going to happen next.

Being vocal in this process is part of advocating for yourself, so be clear about your intentions. Communicate directly to your leader that you're ready for the next step, and set up a meeting to discuss it. Send something to their calendar with a subject line like, "Career Growth and Next Steps," and bring along an agenda similar to the following:

- Review your role expertise and accomplishments.
- Ask what you need to work on to get promoted.
- Build an Individual Development Plan (IDP).
- Discuss timelines and next steps.

**6 POWER MEMO**  Get comfy with confidence!

# THE FEARLESS CAREERIST
## MAKE AMBIGUITY WORK FOR YOU

One of the murkiest parts of the promotion process is the ambiguity that usually surrounds the journey to it. Some organizations have defined paths for their employees, but most aren't this structured. The good news is, you can make this ambiguity work for you. If your company doesn't have a defined "next role" for you, create it!

First, you'll need to consider what your superpowers are, the current needs of the organization, and any gaps there might be in support. The intersection of these is where your elevated role will be. Craft a few bullet points around these and present them to your boss. Tie it in to the company's goals to better explain why this role is needed, and why you're the only person who can fill it.

Approach this conversation confidently, and let them know you're proud of what you've achieved in your role, but that you're ready for a new challenge. Then, ask if they can help you make a plan to get there. If you have a clear vision of where you want to go next, such as a specific title or role, then communicate that. For example, you might say something like, "I'm really proud of my accomplishments in the Marketing Manager role, but I'm ready for the Marketing Director role. Will you help me build a plan to get there?"

If you're unsure about where you want to go next, emphasize your passions and skill set, and in which areas you envision yourself being able to make the most impact.

Be sure to also ask for feedback on what you're excelling at, and what skills or experience they need you to demonstrate to be successful. Ask for some specific examples, and if they can't provide them in the moment, ask them to think it over and follow up with you. Refer to the organization's existing materials, including the job descriptions for your role and the one at the next level, core competencies, skills they value, and so on. Some organizations make more of these available than others, but if yours has them, use them! They're a great source of objectivity because your leader can then just point to the specific skills and examples of what they'd like to see from you.

If you disagree with any of the feedback you receive, recognition of their perspective is a useful tool in your counter dialogue. Provide your own examples to address any of their concerns—after all, this should be a two-way conversation. If your leader consistently can't provide you with any clear feedback and relevant examples, it's their issue, not yours. However, if this prevents you from being promoted, consider reaching out to HR. You might also want to start exploring your options outside of that organization.

What you're looking to gain from this conversation is clarity regarding any skills you need to work on that are holding you back from being promoted. You also want to establish a timeline for making it happen.

If you agree with your boss regarding which skills you need to work on, then it's important that you formalize this by "getting it in writing." Create an Individual Development Plan (IDP) document so the path is clear to both you and your boss. It should specify everything you need to focus on and deliver to get your promotion, including timelines, relevant stakeholders, and examples. It should also include how your boss will take part in this process and witness your development. For example, the skill that you and your boss have mutually decided you need to work on.

Let's say your boss recommends you work on "intentional delegation." An IDP using this example would look something like this:

- **Skills/competency:** Intentional delegation.
- **Implementation plan:** I plan to intentionally delegate aspects of the upcoming Project Pink to various members of the team, based on their skill sets and passions.
- **Key stakeholders:** Bianca, Joy, Sasha, and Gia.
- **Timeline:** Check in with Gia in one month (date).

Make sure you're clear on any timelines and check-in dates with your supervisor. When the time comes to revisit the topic, actively fight any thoughts like, "I don't want to bother my boss—they're so busy." Your promotion is an important conversation that needs to be prioritized, so allow yourself to take up that time and space. This is about you and your career growth, which is incredibly important.

Below are some milestones on your journey to promotion that you can check off and present to your boss during your one-on-one meetings:

- **Say yes to challenging tasks, but don't say yes to everything:** Make sure the majority of what you do take on is impactful to the business—think big, not small.
- **Be a problem solver, not a problem shifter:** If you have a problem at work, be solution-oriented. Go to your boss not only with the problem, but with a potential solution. Problem shifters are less likely to be promoted, as they tend to be viewed as reactive versus proactive.
- **Own your projects from idea, through execution and evaluation:** Being an idea person sets you apart other strong executors. Being innovative is key to being promoted, so always share your ideas and take credit for them. Lead a project from beginning to end, and then present your results. This shows leadership, initiative, and drive.
- **Maintain a future-focused mindset:** Be a visionary, and always tie your vision in with broader company goals.
- **Join strategic task forces and committees:** Tell your boss which meetings you need to be a part of, and then contribute in a meaningful way. This will allow your voice to be heard by those outside your immediate team.

Another important step on the journey to promotion is to have a mentor and be a mentor. Seek out someone who got the promotion you want (or a similar position). This person doesn't have to be at your organization, either.

Keep in mind that mentoring opportunities exist not just upwardly, but also at your job level. These relationships are also important, so be sure to share what you learn from your mentor with some trusted colleagues who you feel would benefit from it. It's a great way to coach your peers and spread knowledge.

Being a mentor is an invigorating experience, and a ton of learning and growth can happen on both sides of the equation. I recommend being a situational mentor, which means you know your specific strengths and skill set, and how to parlay that to others to help them grow.

For example, one of my core superpowers is people-first leadership. Now, I mentor folks who want to learn how to advocate for themselves and/or their teams, get a promotion and/or raise, set boundaries, maintain a good work-life balance, and more. The more you get to know the people in your organization, the more they'll notice your superpowers and seek you out.

\*\*\*

If you follow all of the advice in this chapter, and your boss still isn't on board with promoting you, continuously shuts you down when you try to discuss it, and/or refuses to advocate for you, it's probably time to start looking for a new opportunity.

# PART III
# CULTIVATING

In our final section, we'll build on what we've learned to cultivate our ideal working environment.

First, you'll learn some practical tips for overcoming imposter syndrome—that pesky universal phenomenon that makes us all feel unworthy of our own successes. The more we talk about it, the less menacing it becomes. There are also some potent strategies you can employ when imposter syndrome rears its ugly head that can put you right back on the confidence track.

Next, we'll tackle how to handle conflict at work. In any situation in which people from different backgrounds and walks of life are thrown together, there are going to be disagreements, and the workplace is no different. If this is something you tend to shy away from, we'll break it down into steps just like any other a task so it's far less daunting. After you learn to approach conflict with confidence and control, you'll likely find that it often leads to the most robust discussions and solutions. You might even find (like I did) that you start embracing conflict, rather than viewing it as a chaotic, uncomfortable thing to fear.

You'll also learn how to do one of the best things you can ever do for yourself and your coworkers: implement healthy boundaries.

By the end of this section, you'll have learned how to gain more control over your work environment, so you can make it more of a place you want to be.

# CHAPTER 10
## FIGHTING IMPOSTER SYNDROME

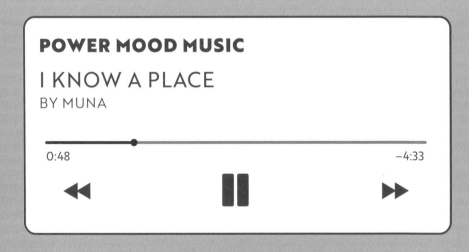

**POWER MOOD MUSIC**

I KNOW A PLACE
BY MUNA

0:48                                          −4:33

Imposter syndrome was first introduced in 1978 by psychologists Pauline Clance and Suzanne Imes. In its simplest form, you experience imposter syndrome when you doubt your abilities, question or diminish your accomplishments, or feel like a fraud. It's something we all experience regardless of age, or our perceived level of success or confidence, but you gotta name it to tame it. The more we talk about it, the more we'll realize we're not alone, and that it's a completely normal and valid feeling.

Luckily, there are tools and strategies you can put in place to push past it. Just because you feel a certain way about yourself doesn't mean that's the whole truth. Frankly, I think we've been duped—is it really a syndrome, or just society telling us which rooms we should and shouldn't be in?

To get past it and see it for what it really is, it's important to recognize where imposter syndrome stems from. It's actually way bigger than you as an individual.

Imposter syndrome comes from a society that repeatedly tells you that you aren't good enough. Men, on the other hand, have been told repeatedly that they belong in boardrooms, and should be leading countries—so they do, and don't even think twice about it. They've never heard otherwise, and the example that's been set for them is a crystal-clear reflection of themselves, so of course, they see themselves leading companies, giving speeches, heading foundations, and running nations.

For women, however, the social narrative looks very different. We don't see ourselves reflected in the boardroom or C-Suite, and when we do, the representation is disproportionately small. Instead, we're asked to take notes in the meeting for the millionth time and denied or passed over for promotions in favor of white men with mediocre skills. When these are the cards you're dealt, it's no wonder that imposter syndrome would persist.

The more we talk about this, though, the less menacing and prevalent it will be. Again, we're all dealing with imposter syndrome, including the seemingly unshakably confident former First Lady, Michelle Obama. In 2020, she discussed the topic in an interview with *Marie Claire*, and advised women to remember that we are our own worst critics.

"The fact is that you wouldn't be in that room if you didn't belong there," Obama told the magazine. "And while negative thoughts are bound to crop up as you take on new roles and challenges, you can acknowledge them without letting them stop you from occupying space and doing the work."

It has helped me immensely to remember that even the "best of the best" of us experience imposter syndrome. When we have the tools to recognize it, we can acknowledge it and move forward.

Below are some of the most common symptoms, so note how many apply to you:

- You struggle to accept compliments.
- You hold yourself to an incredibly high standard.
- You fear making mistakes.
- You downplay your accomplishments, and pass credit on to others.
- You feel you haven't earned your successes.

If you nodded assent to some (or all) of the above, it's time to do something about it!

## FIVE FUNDAMENTAL IMPOSTER SYNDROME ANTIDOTES

If you're struggling with imposter syndrome, there are five handy tools you'll want to have at your disposal to actively combat it whenever it creeps in:

1. **Start (and regularly update) a brag sheet.** We've covered several times how important it is to have one of these, and here's another reason to add to the list. Whenever you're experiencing self-doubt, read your brag sheet to remind yourself of everything you've done to be proud of—both in your work and personal life.

2. **Give yourself permission to be in your feelings and name them.** Again, you gotta name it to tame it. Sometimes, simply articulating a feeling can help you identify and overcome it. For example, if you feel like you don't deserve a certain accolade, talk out the "why." You might have an unfair bias or a super-high standard that you only apply to yourself.

3. **Remember the facts.** Negative thoughts aren't facts. When they creep in, remind yourself who you are, and how hard you've worked to get where you are. You can also try using a positive affirmation, such as, "I am powerful."

4. **Quit the comparison game.** Comparing your journey to someone else's is a dark game that can lead to a downward spiral. What we observe on the outside is almost always not what's actually happening in someone else's reality. Your journey is yours, and it's not replicable.

5. **Talk to a therapist and/or trusted friend.** Don't bottle your feelings and allow them to simmer inside. Talking is healing because it can bring validation. Sometimes, simply saying something out loud is enough to conquer it.

How you talk to yourself matters so much because it's your inner voice that informs how you present yourself to the world. That's why simply reframing negative self-talk is a great way to be proactive and prevent imposter syndrome from creeping in.

Let's look at some examples of negative self-talk, and how you can reframe them as something more positive:

| INSTEAD OF THIS: | SAY THIS: |
|---|---|
| "I'm so stupid for making that mistake." | "I messed up, but that's okay; I'll grow from it." |
| "I can't do this; it's way too hard." | "How can I break this down into smaller steps so I can do it?" |
| "I'm so selfish!" | "It's okay to put myself first sometimes." |

Always keep in mind that *a lot* of high-achieving people experience imposter syndrome. Whenever it happens to you, just remember that you're in very esteemed company.

## THE ART OF ACCEPTING A COMPLIMENT

Whenever someone compliments you on your work, do you normally respond with something like, "Oh yeah, well, it was really a team effort,"?

As we covered earlier in this chapter, struggling to accept compliments is one of the signs of imposter syndrome. This is why, moving forward, you must challenge yourself to graciously accept *all of them*—it will fuel your confidence, both at work and in your personal life.

Next time you receive a compliment on your work, say, "Thanks! I worked hard on that," or, "I appreciate that. I'm really proud of that project." When you accept a compliment, you're not denying others their fair share—you're simply accepting *your* well-earned credit for your contribution. Do so warmly and let it marinate. Yeah, you're awesome!

## FIGHT NEGATIVITY WITH POSITIVITY

Whenever I need a quick, powerful reminder to boost my confidence, I whip out a positive affirmation. To use an affirmation, you can simply say it out loud, write it on a Post-it and stick it to your mirror, text it to yourself, or add it to your brag sheet. You can even make up your own affirmation, if you prefer.

However, if you're an affirmation newbie, any of the following is a good place to start:

- I am powerful.
- I am successful.
- I inspire people through my work.
- I am getting better and better every day.
- Confidence is a choice, and today I choose to be confident.
- I am worthy of what I desire.
- I am enough.

Your power mood is the absolute opposite of imposter syndrome. If you're experiencing any of the following power mood signs, you're well on your way to banishing imposter syndrome for good:

- You regularly celebrate your wins.
- You don't stress when you make a mistake.
- You advocate for yourself.
- You focus on your strengths, rather than your weaknesses.
- You accept compliments eagerly and offer them readily.
- You set boundaries and stick to them.
- You speak with conviction.

\*\*\*

The imposter syndrome phenomenon is way bigger than any of us at an individual level. Society at large is to blame, and it must start to evolve, advance, and do better by those of us who have not been given seats at the table for far too long. And it will only do that if we continue to speak up for ourselves and each other.

We also must fight our own negative inner monologues and talk about imposter syndrome with others whenever it creeps in. When you speak openly about it, you strip it of its potency. Acknowledge it for what it is, but don't let it block your progress. It's only when you champion yourself that you can fully inhabit your power mood!

The chart on the following page can help you start winning the fight against imposter syndrome. Whenever phrases like those in the left column creep into your inner monologue, simply replace them with the Power Mood versions on the right.

| INSTEAD OF THIS: | SAY THIS: |
| --- | --- |
| "I can't do anything right." | "I am learning and growing." |
| "What I do doesn't matter." | "I inspire people through my work." |
| "I'll never learn all of this." | "With practice, this will become easy." |
| "I am out of my depth." | "I will learn from this." |
| "I'll never reach that goal." | "I'm worthy of what I desire." |
| "They are better at this than me." | "What can I learn from them?" |
| "I give up." | "I'll try a different approach." |
| "I messed up." | "This is a learning opportunity." |
| "I wish I had their skills (talent, experience, etc.)." | "I am uniquely skilled." |
| "I am unqualified." | "I am enough." |
| "I'm not working hard enough." | "Rest is productive." |
| "I'm just doing my job." | "I am confident and powerful." |

# CHAPTER 11
## HANDLING CONFLICT

**POWER MOOD MUSIC**

KEEP IT MOVING
BY ALEX NEWELL

0:48                                                     −3:16

C onflict in the workplace is bound to happen. When people of varying personalities and life experiences have to work together to solve problems, conflict will most certainly arise. Workplace conflict has a bad reputation that's unfair and inaccurate.

First, it is standard procedure when working with others, and second, it's actually a good thing. Conflict leads to thoughtful dialogue, which causes ideas to take root and grow. It puts ideas through a pressure test, so they come out the other side a more evolved, stronger version of what they were initially.

Embracing conflict is part of moving up at work. The higher you want to rise, the comfier you need to get with diving head-on into workplace conflict. As a peacekeeping, conflict-averse Libra, this made me so very uncomfortable at first.

However, after some practice stepping well outside my comfort zone, I'm proud to say I now look forward to healthy conflict. I savor the process of hearing people out, asking probing questions, poking holes, asserting my own case, and finding the best path forward as a team. Once you start viewing conflict from a different perspective, you'll be able to do the same.

Some companies deliberately call out the value conflict brings to their workplace. For example, Amazon has sixteen core leadership principles, one of which is, "Have Backbone; Disagree and Commit: Leaders are obligated to respectfully challenge decisions when they disagree, even when doing so is uncomfortable or exhausting. Leaders have conviction and are tenacious. They do not compromise for the sake of social cohesion. Once a decision is determined, they commit wholly."

Workplace conflict is valuable for a number of reasons, but mainly because it gives you (and everyone else) a platform for sharing your unique point of view and encourages innovation. It puts ideas through a vetting process and allows you to analyze potential outcomes. Again, this type of enriching dialogue is what leads to both learning and growth.

Conflict also fosters healthier communication, which leads to a stronger team—nothing causes resentment faster than unresolved conflict.

In her book, *The HBR Guide to Dealing with Conflict*, former management consultant Amy Gallo defined the four different types of conflict:

1. **Task conflict:** What needs to be done?
2. **Process conflict:** How does it need to be done?
3. **Status conflict:** Who needs to do it?
4. **Relationship conflict:** When it gets personal.

Task, process, and status conflict are all quite standard in the workplace. Folks are sure to have different perspectives on what should be done, as well as when, how, and who should do it. If you have a point to make during a conflict, share it, along with your why. There might be times when you don't have a strong POV on a certain issue or project, and that's fine too; let the others hash it out. In those moments when you *do* have a strong opinion on something, though, that's when you want to weigh in.

When dealing with any type of conflict, you can employ the following core strategies to get to the heart of the issue and find solutions:

- **Acknowledge that there *is* a conflict:** Call out the elephant in the room, but make it clear this is a safe space for sharing. Discuss any disagreements openly and encourage active listening. Provide enough time for anyone who wants to share, even it requires scheduling additional meeting time.
- **Brainstorm outcomes:** Discuss the potential positive and/or negative results for all of the various points of view.
- **Determine the best course of action for moving forward:** Even if not all parties agree in the end (which is likely), you can all still commit to moving ahead as a unified team.

In a room full of intelligent and respectful people, conflict can be exciting. Don't take it the wrong way if one of your ideas becomes a source of conflict—that just means it's noteworthy, interesting, and thought-provoking. People want to investigate it from multiple angles. Your idea might evolve and end up in a different place after a healthy discussion, but that's part of the process.

Some workplaces are more conflict-prone than others, and if it happens frequently, it can be mentally and emotionally draining. It's okay to step away from conflict if you just don't have the juice.

Of the four different types, relationship conflict is the most complicated and draining. This is because it's less about the tasks and more about people and their different personalities. In these scenarios, as long as it doesn't cross the line into harassment or discrimination, you might want to seek out a neutral party who can mediate the conversation. This can help you get to the heart of the conflict and ensure that everyone has a chance to be heard.

A recurring conflict I've faced is when a company wants me to achieve better results, but for less money. This is one you might have encountered before, as well. It's when they say something like, "We like what you're doing, but we need you to spend less money from the budget, and get more sales next time." Right. Back here in the real world, it's tough to have your cake and eat it too. This creates conflict because what they're asking for is close to impossible to achieve. However, instead of refusing and storming out of the meeting, embrace the impending conflict and prepare your rebuttal.

In your response, it's a good idea to share the very practical implications of slashing the budget by saying something like, "If we decrease the spending on this, our teams will be significantly less prepared as a result." If they tell you to do it anyway, you've already pointed out the negative impact this will have and can refer back to it later, if necessary. Sometimes, your rebuttal will lead to a much-needed dialogue. On the other hand, if you simply agree to their unrealistic demands, you're setting yourself (and your team) up for failure.

You have to embrace conflict in order to express dissent, and articulate what is and isn't possible. Otherwise, companies will ask you to lasso the moon. Absurd requests like these are your cue to jump in and bring them back to reality.

When you open up a more practical discussion, plausible ideas and solutions can be presented. You'll likely end up meeting in the middle somewhere, which means that's a good compromise. Even if you still disagree with the path forward, you can disagree and commit.

Generally, even if it doesn't end up being the final solution, if you present a thoughtful counter opinion, you'll be respected. The higher-ups tend to appreciate a friendly challenge and conflict is an essential part of doing business.

# CORPORATE CHRONICLES
## HANDLING CONFLICT AT WORK

At one of my prior workplaces, handling conflict was the name of the game, and it was a regular part of my job. However, because it occurred so frequently, I became accustomed to it. I learned when to engage, and when to step back and conserve my energy. After all, I was just doing a job, so there were moments when I thought, "Nah, this isn't worth it."

Whenever I did engage in conflict, it was because I was passionate about my team and their well-being. That's when I would jump in, advocate, and articulate my point of view.

The comfier you get with conflict, the easier it will become. Taking part in robust discussions and seeing the room nod in agreement with your idea or countering argument feels empowering. Moving forward, don't shy away from conflict—embrace it! It will further your leadership skills in a major way.

# CHAPTER 12
## IDENTIFYING AND SETTING HEALTHY BOUNDARIES AT WORK

**POWER MOOD MUSIC**

THE BEST
BY TINA TURNER

0:48                                                          −4:08

◀◀                      ❚❚                      ▶▶

A boundary is where one thing ends and another begins. When it comes to people, our boundaries indicate the limit of what we will or won't tolerate.

Setting boundaries at work is a hot topic of discussion in the career space right now. Several of the videos I've posted about it have gone viral. I freaking love that people are talking about this because employers are being compelled to respond. Unlike back in our parents' day, the intersection of mental health and work is now a large part of the conversation (anyone else still having trouble explaining therapy to their mom, or is that just me?).

Millennials and Gen Zers are at the forefront of the conversation about implementing healthy boundaries at work because we want to lead mentally healthy and balanced lives. We have friends, families, pets, hobbies, freelance gigs, businesses, and a whole life to live outside of our day jobs.

This chapter will help you establish and maintain healthier boundaries between your work life and, well, life.

I've never liked the phrase "work-life balance" because it's clunky and truly backward. Why does work get to come first? I don't think so, honey! That's just another societal mindset that needs to shift. It should be something like "prioritizing life" or "life-before-work realism." In her brilliant book, *Lead from the Outside*, Stacey Abrams' describes it as "work-life Jenga," which is incredibly accurate. If you've ever played the game, you know the entire objective is to make as many moves as you can without causing the whole thing to collapse.

The reality is, work can't (and shouldn't) be be your number-one priority all of the time. For me, work is an important part of my life, but it's not the center of it. It's important to remember that your job isn't your life, but just part of it. Maybe it's a really important part of your life and maybe it isn't. For some folks, it's just a means to an end—what you have to do to support yourself and your family. Either way, we all also exist outside of it and are so much more than our jobs.

Companies are looking out for themselves (a.k.a., the money), and you need to do the same. They're in the business of protecting their business, but you need to be in the business of protecting *you*.

## THE FEARLESS CAREERIST
### UNAPOLOGETIC BOUNDARIES

You should never, ever apologize for having boundaries of any kind, but especially in the workplace, so erase "sorry" from your narrative when it comes to this. Apologizing for a boundary implies that you've wronged someone, and you certainly haven't.

Next time you're tempted to say something like, "I'm sorry I can't stay and help more with this project," replace it with, "I have to head out now. I'll work more on this project on Thursday."

Setting boundaries is applicable in every industry and every role. Currently, it's more accepted in some industries than others, but that doesn't mean you can't pave the way. Even if you've found an organization that you trust that also takes care of you, it's still imperative to set healthy boundaries. No job or salary is worth sacrificing your mental health, and setting boundaries is burnout prevention 101.

Before you can set healthy boundaries at work, though, you have to figure out what they are.

## IDENTIFY

To set personal boundaries, you first have to occupy a state of mind in which you put yourself first. This will likely require you to let go of certain notions, such as the idea that other people's feelings and reactions are your responsibility. If you're a consummate people-pleaser, this chapter will be very important for you because it will challenge you to actively push against your natural tendency to put others' needs before your own.

However, once you get used to prioritizing your needs, the positive life changes you'll experience will speak for themselves. It's time to channel your power mood and grant yourself full permission to put yourself first! This will allow you to identify and set your boundaries, and it's one of the best things you'll ever do for yourself.

Boundaries apply in both your personal and professional life. Once you get in the habit of using them, you'll be able to seamlessly enact them in all areas of your life, including with your family, partner, friends, boss, coworkers, etc. Once you've given yourself permission to prioritize your well-being, you'll realize that you can, in fact, set boundaries and still be a high-achiever at work (is your mind blown?).

There are five types of boundaries to consider when it comes to your working life:

1. **Physical boundaries:** These refer specifically to physical contact in the workplace. Are you okay with shaking hands, high fives, and hugs? Or, like me, would you prefer no one touch you at all? Either is fine, you just need to define what you are and are not okay with. Anything that makes you even slightly uncomfortable is a boundary.

2. **Emotional boundaries:** These involve anything that requires any type of emotional labor from you, such as talking about your relationship, family, politics, religion, sexual orientation, race, and so on. Identify any topics that stress you out or exhaust you—those are your no-go's.

3. **Communication boundaries:** How do you prefer your coworkers to communicate with you about work? Is email fine, or do you prefer a messaging app, like Slack or Teams? One of my boundaries is I do not give out my personal cell number at work, but you might be fine with folks calling you. Again, you draw the line at whatever makes you feel uncomfortable.

4. **Time boundaries:** This involves limiting your work hours, including when you're available to connect with colleagues. A lot of jobs now offer more flexibility here, so it's helpful to consider at what time of day you're most productive. Do you prefer to start earlier so you can end earlier, or would you rather sleep in a bit? Define what your workday looks like, and don't forget to include some breaks. And always use *all* of your paid time off; it's part of your compensation.

5. **Workload boundaries:** Know your expertise and where you add value. Sometimes, your boss or others might attempt to delegate something to you that's not within the scope of your role. This is another instance in which knowing your

job description really comes in handy. Listen to your gut, and you'll know when your plate is approaching full—you want to implement this boundary well before you get to that point.

**7** **POWER MEMO**

Setting boundaries isn't selfish. It sets both you and the organization up for success by strategically positioning you to deliver your best work.

Throughout your career, and sometimes, even at the same job, your boundaries will shift and evolve. You'll find that you have both hard and soft boundaries. A hard boundary might be your working hours, while a soft one might be the types of projects you take on.

For example, you don't want to take on too much, but if you're at a stage in your career where you'd like a promotion, you might take on a project that you normally wouldn't. If it's something that will show off your skills and help you grow, you might soften your project boundary. However, softening it doesn't mean it's gone—don't burn yourself out over it. You might have to deprioritize other work to take on a "stretch" project like this.

Only you can decide which of your boundaries are hard, and which are soft. However, in both life and work, you don't want to have too many soft boundaries, or you open yourself up to be taken advantage of. It's about striking a balance between what you absolutely won't compromise on and the types of opportunities you'd be open to if they'll provide strategic growth.

This might sound controversial, but you shouldn't be giving 100 percent every single day at work; space it out, based on how you feel. Some days, you might feel like giving 90 to 100 percent, but on others, you might only have 50 to 80 percent in your tank. Give yourself permission not to fire on all cylinders every single moment of every day—that's a recipe for burnout.

And on those days where you can't give anything? That's when you use up that personal or vacation time. You have a life to live outside of work, so make sure you're spending some of your precious energy on you.

## COMMUNICATE

You can't put your boundaries into practice and maintain them until you've communicated them. After all, if no one knows they exist, they'll overstep and cross them all the time. The process of communicating your workplace boundaries should start during the interview process. Certain companies are more accepting of them than others, and you want to spot which camp they're in right away. An organization that has zero respect for its employees' boundaries doesn't deserve your talent.

You can initiate the boundaries conversation during a job interview by asking some of the following curious questions:

- What are the typical working hours for this role?
- Is there an expectation to answer emails after hours?
- What do you love about working here?
- Do folks on the team typically take all of their vacation time?
- How does this company help its employees maintain a good life-work balance?
- What benefits do you offer that are centered around life-work balance?

You can also ask the interviewer what *their* communication and time boundaries are, and that will open up the door for you to share yours. As you get closer to the final round of interviews, it's pretty standard to meet with someone on the actual team you'd be working on who also reports to your potential future boss. This is the perfect opportunity to ask a few more probing questions about a company's attitude toward boundaries.

I wouldn't recommend joining a team without speaking to at least one person who's already on it. If a company doesn't schedule a conversation for you like this, you can ask them to do so.

## SIGNS THAT A COMPANY WON'T RESPECT YOUR BOUNDARIES

If you notice any of the following red flags during a job interview, they are clear signs that this company has zero respect for boundaries, and you should probably flee immediately:

- **They ask personal, irrelevant, or even illegal questions:** These can include anything personal, such as your marital status, whether you plan to start a family soon, your religious beliefs, and so on.
- **They evade your questions about life-work balance:** Or, they respond with something like, "We work very hard here and are looking for people who are willing to make sacrifices and do the same." This means they plan to take advantage of you.
- **The job description and/or list of duties are vague:** This leaves way too much room for interpretation and puts you at high risk for burnout.
- **They pressure you to schedule an interview or respond to an offer quickly:** Both are indications that they have a high employee turnover.
- **They ask you to do a bunch of unpaid labor during the interview process:** Some companies will ask you to create a presentation or take some sort of test to assess your skills. However, if it would take you more than an hour to complete and/or seems excessive, it's likely a sign they won't respect your time.
- **No one you meet has been at the company very long:** This is another sign that people are jumping ship quickly.
- **Everyone you meet is in a bad mood, exhausted, or burnt out:** This indicates employee morale is universally low.

- **The hiring manager won't introduce you to anyone on the team:** As I mentioned earlier, this is a very common step in the interview process these days. If they block you from doing this, it's a pretty clear indication that they don't trust what someone on the team might say about the company and/or its leadership.
- **They refer to the team as "family":** This is usually an indication that they'll expect you to do a lot more than they pay you to do. The word "family" is used to mirror a bond that often transcends boundaries. Work colleagues *are not* your family, and a good company both acknowledges and respects your *real* one.

It's absolutely necessary that you communicate your boundaries to everyone with whom you'll be working most often, such as your peers and supervisors. But how can you do that effectively? Let's take a look!

## CORPORATE CHRONICLES
### THE "FAMILY" RED FLAG

Companies that describe their employees as "family" usually do so to infer that they care, while simultaneously exploiting their staff. I once worked at such a place and, in the beginning, it wasn't a problem. However, red flags soon started to appear. They expected the work we delivered to be of the highest quality, but also to be finished yesterday, while paying everyone the bare minimum. Additionally, they provided few (if any) resources to help us accomplish all of this work.

They stampeded over all of my boundaries, while proclaiming, "but we're family here!" Well, only if that family is incredibly unhealthy! Just like a toxic relative, most companies that refer to their employees this way will take advantage of them and consistently violate their boundaries. They expected way too much of me and gave very little in return. I'm sure this isn't true, of every organization that slips "family" into the conversation, but I would still recommend you proceed with caution if you encounter this in the wild.

## HOW TO COMMUNICATE YOUR BOUNDARIES

Sometimes, it can be difficult to find the right language to communicate a boundary. It feels uncomfy at first, but it will become easier over time. In fact, eventually, it morphs into power. All of these techniques are best employed when starting a new job, but you can also implement them at your current job. Just keep in mind, if your current workplace is an "antiboundaries" type of organization, you're going to have to expend a lot of time and energy communicating and restating what yours are.

Here's some specific language you can use to communicate different types of boundaries:

- **Physical boundaries:** If someone goes in for an unwanted hug, just say, "I'm more comfortable with this," and then present your hand for a shake. Or, you can simply say, "No thanks, but it's great to see you!"
- **Emotional boundaries:** If someone asks a question about your personal life you don't want to answer, you can just say something like, "I prefer not to talk about that at work; it's a boundary of mine."
- **Communication boundaries:** If someone asks for your cell phone number, you might say, "I prefer email. It's the best way to reach me." And if someone messages you after working hours, do not respond—this will immediately establish your boundary.
- **Time boundaries:** If someone schedules a meeting on your calendar for 5:30 p.m. and your workday ends at 5 p.m., decline and suggest a few alternative times that work for you.
- **Workload boundaries:** When your boss assigns you more work and your plate is already full, you might ask something like, "Can you help me deprioritize some of these other projects if this one is urgent?" If the task is outside your job description, you could say, "My skill set and role aren't well-suited to this project. Is there someone else who could tackle it?" This is more effective with bosses than, "I have too much on my plate right now," even when that's the truth.

Many people that you encounter in your career will make things that are not urgent at all seem like the end of the world. Unless you work in medicine, whatever is being asked of you can most likely wait until a bit later, or tomorrow, or next week. You don't want to set a precedent of responding immediately to everything, or after working hours. This will just encourage those people to continue pinging you about every little thing at all hours. The best course of action in that situation is to simply not respond until you are back at work.

As remote work has become a lot more common, boundaries are more important than ever because the line between home and work can quickly become blurred. If you finish your workday at 5 p.m., then close that laptop at exactly that time each day. They're not paying you to work any later than that, so don't.

## MAINTAIN

Maintaining your boundaries is a long-term enterprise, but it's often easier than identifying and communicating them. After you've set and communicated them, below are some best practices for maintaining your workplace boundaries:

- **Ensure there's an agenda for every meeting:** Whether you're leading it yourself or just attending, a clear agenda can help protect your time boundary.
- **Use the "Out of Office" feature:** Set up automated email responses whenever you're out of the office so people won't expect a response from you.

- **Use the "Do Not Disturb" feature:** When you're busy or in go-mode, set your Slack, Teams, or any other messaging program's status to "Do Not Disturb." This will protect both your time and workload boundaries.
- **Don't immediately accept projects outside your scope:** Instead, communicate your concerns and/or recommend someone else who would be better suited for the task.

Identifying, communicating, and maintaining boundaries can be difficult, but it's also incredibly empowering. Yes, others will attempt to violate your boundaries, but remember, this is why you implemented them in the first place. It's a good idea to prepare a consistent response to use whenever this happens. This will help both you and the other person build good habits. Plus, your reinforcement will help them better understand your needs.

First, though, whenever someone violates one of your boundaries, try not to take it personally. They might be unfamiliar with the idea of boundaries in general, or they simply might not know this was one of yours.

Next, be sure to restate (reinforce) your boundary and there's no need to go into too much detail. For example, instead of saying, "So sorry I can't come to the team outing tonight. I'm super exhausted and have way too much going on, but I'll definitely be at the next one," try, "I'm not able to attend tonight. Enjoy!" You don't owe anyone an explanation—your boundary is simply your boundary.

Finally, if the situation calls for it, you can also offer alternatives. This shows that you're a team player who can also maintain boundaries. For example, if someone asks you for help on something when you're extremely busy, you could respond with something like, "I'd like to help, but I'm currently at capacity. I can contribute to your project at the end of next week."

If your boundaries are repeatedly being tested and/or crossed, it might be time to have a conversation with the perpetrator. Explain that their approach is impacting you negatively, and then restate your boundaries and why they are important.

This can be really tough when the perpetrator is your boss. You'll have to decide if such a conversation is worth your energy and has the possibility of being fruitful. However, if the answer is a hard no, it's probably time to move on from working for them. If you think there's hope, though, open up a dialogue. Be crystal clear about what you need and your current challenges, and clarify that your work quality will continue to be high. You should also be prepared to negotiate with them. Keep the conversation framed around the fact that you need to be in a position to deliver your best work, and you need them to be your partner in that.

## INSPIRE

While it isn't a required step in the boundary-setting process, inspiration is what occurs organically *after* you follow the steps we outlined above. Inspiring others to set their own healthy boundaries is the ultimate by-product of setting your own. In some cases, you won't be the first person at your workplace to have boundaries. If you're lucky, many before you will have already done so and set a precedent. Many of us, though, will have to be trailblazers—the first person on the team or at an organization to ever even mention boundaries.

I once had a job in an industry where boundary-setting was basically unheard of at the time. I saw my supervisors burning out quickly and knew I didn't want to end up there. So, I started implementing boundaries for the sake of my rapidly deteriorating mental health. I made no apologies, nor did I offer any long explanations. I simply set my boundaries, communicated them, restated them if they were crossed, and continued to deliver great work.

My teammates and colleagues noticed this, and it inspired them to do the same. In fact, we often talked about how beneficial and life-altering it was. It didn't make our jobs instantly perfect, but it was still a major life improvement and became a cornerstone of our team's culture. As a result, our morale was high, folks were motivated, and turnover was extremely low.

Sometimes, you have to be the first person to do something and get the ball rolling. So, set the bar high, implement some healthy boundaries, and watch others follow your lead.

*\*\**

It can take some time to define what your boundaries are, but this can be a beautiful way to get to know yourself. So, take some time to think about what matters most to you and what you need to be fulfilled.

Once you've set and communicated your boundaries, you'll get tired real fast of having to restate them whenever they're crossed, but make sure that you always do. It does get easier! By the time I became a manager, I felt far more empowered to set boundaries. As a director, I've found that my boundaries set an excellent example for my team.

So, again, you should never feel selfish for having boundaries. Not only do they ensure that you can deliver your best work, but they also protect your mental health, and will encourage others to do the same!

# CHAPTER 13

## PEOPLE-FIRST LEADERSHIP

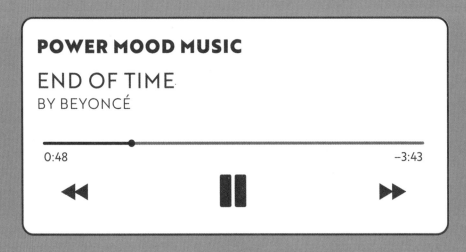

**POWER MOOD MUSIC**

END OF TIME
BY BEYONCÉ

0:48                                                    −3:43

The thing they don't tell you about becoming a manager, director, vice president, or CEO is that it's not necessarily about who's the best at the technical aspects of the job—it's all about your people skills.

Are you an inspiring visionary? Do you understand what motivates people, and know how to bring out the best in others? The best managers do, and the higher you rise in the corporate ranks, the more your people prowess will matter.

I truly hope that those who will benefit the most from this chapter find their way to it. (To any of you out there with a toxic boss, open the book to this chapter and slide it under their office door.)

If you want to rise through the ranks in your career, everything we've covered thus far is absolutely necessary, but getting folks to *want* to follow you is mandatory. Even if that's not your forté (hi, introverts!), these tips can help you vastly improve your people skills.

Corporate America doesn't do a great job of training managers to actually lead people. As a result, most of them are absolutely clueless on that front. Very few companies actually take the time to train their managers in how to be empathetic, inclusive, and motivational. Instead, they just thrust the person with the most experience in the technical aspects of the role into a leadership position, whether they have any people skills or not.

If you want to rise through the ranks in your career, everything we've covered thus far is absolutely necessary, but getting folks to want to follow you is mandatory. Even if that's not your forté (hi, introverts), these tips can help you vastly improve your people skills.

And way too often, this person doesn't have any skills in that area at all. This is one of the major reasons so many people end up quitting bad bosses; they simply weren't trained at all in how to lead. Being great at marketing doesn't automatically make you great at managing a *team* of marketers. It's an entirely different skill set.

To put it simply, to be a great manager, you have to put your people first. They come before all your tasks, deadlines, and meetings. This is a foundational aspect of leadership. If you prioritize your team, positive results will follow. If your people are happy and motivated, they'll be in a position to deliver their best work.

People-first leadership could be an entire book on its own (which I might need to write one day!). But in this chapter, I'll give you an overview of the core principles: building trust, celebrating strengths, and elevating your team.

## BUILDING TRUST

If you're promoted to a leadership role, you'll most likely be leading some of your former peers. If you're hired in from the outside, you won't know anyone on the team. In either situation, building trust is paramount to your success. Again, what many people want most is just to be heard. Your team will want to know that you're willing to listen to them, and that you're on their side.

When you're a new manager, be sure to set up one-on-ones with each person on your team. This will give you a chance to get to know them a bit, and for them to get to know you. Be sure to ask them what their superpowers are, as well as their short- and long-term goals. Find out what their current priority projects are. You can also ask them their preferred methods of communication and what their boundaries are

The best leaders are both allies and advocates on their employees' journey to success. Let them know from day one that you're on their side and want to support their upward mobility. You should share your boundaries, as well, and do so first, so they'll feel more comfortable about sharing theirs. They'll likely find this refreshing, transparent, and real. The first time I initiated this dialogue with my team, some were surprised, but in the best way possible.

Whenever they hear a new leader is coming in, most people are immediately suspicious and put their guard up. If you want to get them on your side from the jump, just talk about your boundaries and encourage them to set some of their own.

I'm a fan of starting all team meetings with an engaging discussion. Another a fun way to kick off a meeting is by sharing your core working values with your team, and asking them to do the same. For example, I can't do my best work without creativity, flexibility, empathy, and humor. This particular exercise gets people thinking about what matters most to them and what they need to deliver their best. And again, people love to talk about themselves, so it's a win-win!

Also, let them know that you're always available to hear their questions, feedback, concerns, and stressors. They need to know your door is open; if you seem unavailable, frustration could start to brew. As their leader, you *want* to hear about any challenges so you can address them before it's too late.

I frequently reiterated to my team that if anyone needed to talk, they should feel free to add time to my calendar outside of our scheduled one-on-ones, or send me a message. I also made it clear that I would not be criticizing them for mistakes. Rather, I'd be there to talk them through it when it happens so we can all learn and grow together.

I made it very clear that they were my priority. This not only established trust, but also led to strong working relationships, high team morale, fantastic results and impact on the business, and extremely low turnover. Micromanagers, Antisocial Tyrants, and Blame Shovelers, take note: being a people-first leader works for your people, and it's also a joy to be one.

Building trust is an ongoing process. It takes much more than the initial one-on-one meeting, so ensure that you have regular connections set up with all your team members and be an active listener. A great item to add to your recurring agendas is "Start, Stop, Continue." This is where you ask your team members what they'd like for you to start doing, stop doing, and continue doing as a leader to help them succeed. It opens the door and allows them to offer informal feedback, and I strongly recommend it. It leads to a lot of meaningful conversations.

Establish and build a culture of empathy and support within your team by encouraging folks to take mental health days off and set the example yourself. Take mental health days, work standard hours, don't respond to emails on the weekend, take your vacation time, and so on. Adhering to your own boundaries will be inspiring and set a strong example for your team.

When it comes to current events, don't ignore, explore. Acknowledge what's going on in the world—positive and negative— offer an empathetic ear, communicate the message that there's so much more to life than this job and its associated tasks. Sometimes, it feels like the world is crumbling around us, and we need to hear that it's okay to take a break, a mental health day, or a vacation. Work is not the be-all, end-all.

Teams appreciate a boss who understands and expresses this. The rise of remote work has also led to an *increase* in productivity. People want to eliminate lengthy, draining commutes. Remote or hybrid work situations give people the flexibility they need to do their jobs well, on their terms. And if they're delivering great work, why place restrictions around it?

## CULTIVATE A SAFE SPACE FOR YOUR TEAM

When meeting new people in interviews or meetings, share your pronouns. Again, this opens the door for them to share theirs if they choose. It's also important to be flexible and adjust your leadership style according to the needs of the individual. A one-size-fits-all approach isn't effective if you want to be a people-first leader. Also, be sure to show appreciation for your team. Give shout-outs often, and offer words of affirmation and encouragement more than constructive criticism.

Actively create space for idea-sharing, brainstorming, and discussion, and ensure that everyone has an opportunity to share. Take the time to learn the personality types and working styles of your team. You can make it a group activity and ask everyone to take an assessment, such as the Myers-Briggs Type Indicator (MBTI), Strengths Finder, Predictive Index, and so on. This allows you and everyone else to discover their strengths and can offer fresh perspectives.

# CELEBRATE STRENGTHS

Many leaders spend way too much time harping on their team members' weaknesses, and how they can improve. Constructive criticism can be helpful, but it should never outweigh celebrating strengths.

When you articulate and praise someone's superpowers, it makes them feel seen and powerful. Plus, you unlock the ability to channel their specific superpowers into the best possible results for the team and business. This makes people feel amazing and produces results. You'll look great and so will your team, which makes your job much easier.

Having a team with diverse strengths is important, so as you identify the superpowers of those on your team, note any skill gaps and hire accordingly. You need folks from diverse backgrounds who have had diverse experiences, including all races, genders, sexualities, socioeconomic backgrounds, and those with disabilities.

The following statistics show exactly how much a diverse team can improve a workplace:

- A study by Boston Consulting Group found that diverse management teams lead to 19 percent higher revenues.
- McKinsey & Company found that diverse and inclusive corporations are 35 percent more likely to outperform their competitors.
- Clear Company reported in early 2022 that companies employing an equal number of men and women produce up to 41 percent higher revenue.
- A study at Deloitte University found that millennials are 83 percent more likely to be engaged when they work at inclusive companies.

Inclusive leadership doesn't end at hiring diversely. You also need to elevate diverse voices in meetings, and speak up if you witness any micro- or macroaggressions, or harassment. Do your best to promote qualified women to higher-level roles, especially the Black and Latina women on your team.

# ELEVATE

Now that you've built trust and regularly celebrate your team's unique strengths, it's time to put your money where your mouth is. It's your responsibility as a people-first leader to promote the folks on your team to the next level.

I once worked for someone who didn't want to promote me because they thought I might be a threat to their own hard-earned status. This attitude is harmful, backward, and incorrect. By holding me back, they were doing the same to themselves. We all rise and are stronger together, and, as a leader, there's no truer testament to my leadership than promoting my people. A leader who fosters *more* great leaders is incredibly valuable.

To elevate your team, you first need to encourage them to promote their work (see chapter 9), and you should do so, as well. Again, a good boss is their team's strongest ally and fiercest advocate. Highlight their ideas, projects, and results to the powers that be. It needs to come from you, and you need to start building their case for promotion well in advance, so don't miss out on any opportunities to herald them. When your team shines, you shine too.

When I worked in a very male-dominated workplace, I made it my personal mission to hire, elevate, and promote as many women as I could, and especially women of color. I'd noticed that men were being hired and promoted at an incredibly high rate, but women were not.

To address the issue, I first spoke about it with other female leaders at the company, and found that we were all frustrated about it. After we discussed it and united, we really started to get somewhere—again, we're always more powerful as a collective. This is a fantastic and powerful way to infiltrate from within and change the system for the better.

Great leaders extend their power mood to others, and when your team witnesses yours, they'll be inspired! You'll be arming the next generation of leaders with the tools they need to advocate for themselves and elevate others—and what a powerful legacy that is.

# TAKEAWAYS AND FINAL THOUGHTS

**POWER MOOD MUSIC**

BLOW OUT MY CANDLE
BY BETTY WHO

0:48                                           −2:59

It's time to celebrate! By reading this book, you've invested in yourself! From now on, you'll be able to own your accomplishments, land that dream job, and ask for more. The curtain is rising and you're taking the stage; your power mood era has begun!

Whenever you need a boost or reminder of what to do next, just review these vital gold nuggets to stay on track:

- **Confidence is a decision:** We choose the moments in which we need to conjure it.
- **Know your superpowers:** Call attention to them whenever possible and make sure your boss knows what they are.
- **Be compelling, clear, and take credit for your work:** Do this on your resume *and* in person.
- **An interview is a conversation, not an interrogation:** If any question makes you feel uncomfortable, that's a major red flag. Call it out, and ask what that has to do with your ability to perform the job.
- **A negotiation is a collaboration, not a confrontation:** Remember that "no" is where it all begins.
- **Be intentional with your apologies at work:** Cut out any excessive "sorries."
- **It's okay to quit a toxic job:** Listen to your gut, and know that you deserve better.
- **Advocating for yourself is the fastest route to promotion:** No one else is going to do it for you.
- **Negative thoughts are just that:** They're *not* facts.
- **Don't shy away from conflict:** On the contrary, embrace it! It leads to solutions (and respect).
- **Setting boundaries isn't selfish:** They're a necessity to cultivate a healthy work-life balance.

It's impossible to overstate the incredible results women can achieve when we come together.

Always remember that together, we are incendiary!

# REFERENCES

Abrams, Stacey. *Lead from the Outside: How to Build Your Future and Make Real Change*. New York: Henry Holt and Co./Macmillan, 2018.

Adams, Olivia. "Michelle Obama Shares Tips for Tackling Imposter Syndrome at Work." *Marie Claire*, November 3, 2020. Marieclaire.co.uk/news/celebrity-news/michelle-obama-imposter-syndrome-689340.

Amazon Jobs. n.d. "Leadership Principles." Amazon.jobs/en/principles. Accessed: July 28, 2022.

Clance, Pauline Rose and Imes, Suzanne Ament. "The Imposter Phenomenon in High Achieving Women: Dynamics and Therapeutic Intervention." *Psychotherapy: Theory, Research, & Practice*, 1978. Paulineroseclance.com/pdf/ip_high_achieving_women.pdf.

Freyd, Jennifer J. n.d. "What is DARVO?" Freyd Dynamics Lab, University of Oregon. Dynamic.uoregon.edu/jjf/defineDARVO.html. Accessed July 28, 2022.

Gallo, Amy. *HBR Guide to Dealing with Conflict*. Boston: Harvard Business Review Press, 2017.

Gallup. "State of the American Manager Report." 2015. Gallup.com/services/182216/state-american-manager-report.aspx?.

Heilman, Madeline E. "Gender Stereotypes and Workplace Bias." *Research in Organizational Behavior*, November 21, 2012. sciencedirect.com/science/article/abs/pii/S0191308512000093.

Hunt, Vivian *et al.* "Why Diversity Matters." McKinsey & Company. January 1, 2015. Mckinsey.com/business-functions/people-and-organizational-performance/our-insights/why-diversity-matters.

King, Brittany K. "The State of Women in the Workplace, 2021." Lorman. March 8, 2021. Lorman.com/blog/post/women-in-the-workplace-2021.

Levitsky, Allison. "Job-Hoppers Are Snagging 30% Raises." Protocol. February 28, 2022. Protocol.com/bulletins/job-hoppers-pay-bumps.

Lorenzo, Rocío, *et al.* "How Diverse Leadership Teams Boost Innovation." Boston Consulting Group. January 23, 2018. Bcg.com/publications/2018/how-diverse-leadership-teams-boost-innovation.

Menzies, Felicity. n.d. "Gender Bias at Work: The Assertiveness Double-Bind." Include-Empower.com. Accessed July 28, 2022. Cultureplusconsulting.com/2018/03/10/gender-bias-work-assertiveness-double-bind.

Mohr, Tara Sophia. "Why Women Don't Apply for Jobs Unless They're 100% Qualified." *Harvard Business Review*, August 25, 2014.

Parker, Kim. "What's Behind the Growing Gap Between Men and Women in College Completion?" Pew Research Center. November 8, 2021. Pewresearch.org/fact-tank/2021/11/08/whats-behind-the-growing-gap-between-men-and-women-in-college-completion/

Prooker, Brijana. "It's Time for Women to Break Up with Politeness." *Elle*. April 14, 2021. Elle.com/culture/a35854625/no-more-politeness-2021.

Robert Half Talent Solutions. "Who Tried to Negotiate Salary?" February 5, 2018. Roberthalf.com/blog/compensation-and-benefits/who-most-likely-negotiated-salary.

Schmidt, Claire. "6 Statistics to Better Understand the Extent of Discrimination in the Workplace." Nasdaq, March 2, 2022. Nasdaq.com/articles/6-statistics-to-better-understand-the-extent-of-discrimination-in-the-workplace.

Schumann, Karina, *et al.* "Why Women Apologize More Than Men: Gender Differences in Thresholds for Perceiving Offensive Behavior." *Psychological Science*, September 20, 2010. Pubmed.ncbi.nlm.nih.gov/20855900.

Smith, Christie, *et al.*. "The Radical Transformation of Diversity and Inclusion: The Millennial Influence." Deloitte Consulting LLP. 2015. Deloitte.com/content/dam/Deloitte/us/Documents/about-deloitte/us-inclus-millennial-influence-120215.pdf.

Staley, Oliver. "When to Switch Jobs to Get the Biggest Salary Increase." Quartz. April 21, 2016. Qz.com/666915/when-to-switch-jobs-to-get-the-biggest-salary-increase.

U.S. Census Bureau. "PINC-05. Work Experience-People 15 Years Old and Over, by Total Money Earnings, Age, Race, Hispanic Origin, Sex, and Disability Status." 2020. Census.gov.

U.S. Department of Labor, Bureau of Labor Statistics. "The Employment Situation—July 2022." August 5, 2022. bls.gov/news.release/pdf/empsit.pdf.

Wholley, Meredith. "12 Workplace Diversity Statistics You Should Know in 2022." Clear Company. February 1, 2022. Blog.clearcompany.com/12-workplace-diversity-statistics.

# ACKNOWLEDGMENTS

It's been a lifelong goal of mine to write a book, and I truly can't believe I'm sitting here typing these acknowledgements. I have some very important folks to thank who took care of me along this journey, and generously provided many late-night texts, major emotional support, and lots of snacks—for all of that, I am forever grateful.

To the powerfully assertive, independent, beautiful women in my family: Toni, Meg, Cam, Mom, and Grandma Marge, thank you for your encouragement, enthusiasm, and love. To my Grandma Jo, I know you are proud and it means the world! Dad, thank you for setting a great example of resilience and strength. I've always felt supported by you, and I love you so much! We are both writers now.

Rae Rae, thank you for being my guiding star throughout this process and in my life. I appreciate your honesty, eagerness to listen, and your commitment to championing the people you love. Now it's my turn to champion you—the queen of reading, the fearless founder of our precious book club, and one of my all-time forever faves—thank you for your friendship.

A standing ovation for Meredith for inspiring me on an everyday basis. You are the epitome of a people-first leader, and I've learned so much of what I know from you. Your generosity, loyalty, love, and unwavering motivation are unmatched. Let's never stop growing, seeing shows, and eating all of NYC's finest foods.

Andrew, thank you for your vital sharp opinions, multi-industry know-how, and steadfast support. Your distinctive perspectives have made me a stronger a writer, business owner, and person. Gil, I truly appreciate you for always being hyped and encouraging, texting back, chopping it up, and providing your thoughtful notes— it is a continued privilege to be your bestie. Shoutout to my book club babes and fabulous friends, Anna and Pat, for the boundless empowerment, meaningful conversation, and gossip.

To my dear friend Fer, thank you for being the inspiring, hilarious, supportive legend that you always are and a true queen among queens. I'm honored to recognize Megan and Brad for introducing me to the *Las Cultch* podcast, which truly informed the energy I channeled and proudly occupied throughout this writing.

Major thanks and props to my literary agent, Rachel Cone-Gorham, for your expert guidance, encouragement, and fierce advocacy. A massive thank you to Rage, Amanda, Lydia, and the entire team at Quarto for believing in this book and sharing in my enthusiasm. It's an honor to work with a team of badass, like-minded women.

Finally, to the power mood community of gals and nonbinary pals, you are the reason this book exists. I am inspired by you every day. Thank you for your encouragement, radiant energy, and eagerness to challenge the system. I am so proud of you!

Sam

# ABOUT THE AUTHOR

Sam DeMase is a Career Confidence Coach and Self-Advocacy Expert with a community of over 400,000 followers on social media (@apowermood on Instagram). She is known for her direct, actionable tips on how to hack the corporate system. When she's not fighting the patriarchy, you can find her sipping green tea at home in Brooklyn, New York, seeing every Broadway musical, and blasting '90s pop divas.

© Carly Piersol